Sensory Stories for Children and Teens
with Special Educational Needs

of related interest

Practical Sensory Programmes
For Students with Autism Spectrum Disorder
and Other Special Needs
Sue Larkey
ISBN 978 1 84310 479 7
eISBN 978 1 84642 567 7

Sensory Stimulation
Sensory-Focused Activities for People
with Physical and Multiple Disabilities
Susan Fowler
Foreword by Hilary Johnson
ISBN 978 1 84310 455 1
eISBN 978 1 84642 576 9

**Simple Low-Cost Games and
Activities for Sensorimotor Learning**
A Sourcebook of Ideas for Young Children
Including Those with Autism, ADHD, Sensory Processing
Disorder, and Other Learning Differences
Lisa A. Kurtz
ISBN 978 1 84905 977 0
eISBN 978 0 85700 879 4

**Speak, Move, Play and Learn with
Children on the Autism Spectrum**
Activities to Boost Communication Skills,
Sensory Integration and Coordination Using Simple Ideas
from Speech and Language Pathology and Occupational Therapy
Lois Jean Brady, America X Gonzalez, Maciej Zawadzki and Corinda Presley
Illustrated by Byron Roy James
ISBN 978 1 84905 872 8
eISBN 978 0 85700 531 1

**Fuzzy Buzzy Groups for Children with Developmental
and Sensory Processing Difficulties**
A Step-by-Step Resource
Fiona Brownlee and Lindsay Munro
Illustrated by Aisling Nolan
ISBN 978 1 84310 966 2
eISBN 978 0 85700 194 8

SENSORY STORIES

for Children and Teens with Special Educational Needs

A PRACTICAL GUIDE

Joanna Grace

Foreword by Flo Longhorn

Jessica Kingsley *Publishers*
London and Philadelphia

First published in 2015
by Jessica Kingsley Publishers
73 Collier Street
London N1 9BE, UK
and
400 Market Street, Suite 400
Philadelphia, PA 19106, USA

www.jkp.com

Library of Congress Cataloging in Publication Data
A CIP catalog record for this book is available from the Library of Congress

British Library Cataloguing in Publication Data
A CIP catalogue record for this book is available from the British Library

ISBN 978 1 84905 484 3
eISBN 978 0 85700 874 9

Printed and bound in Great Britain

MIX
Paper from
responsible sources
FSC® C013604

This book is dedicated to the backers of the Sensory Story Project

Contents

PART III USING SENSORY STORIES TO FORM THE BASIS OF GROUP SESSIONS

PART IV ASSESSMENT

FOREWORD

This book tells a sensory story. It is for the seeker of sensory knowledge, looking for substantial ideas with which to plunge into new worlds of sensory storytelling. Each chapter offers a wealth of ideas and knowledge including themes and ideas that could be placed at the core of a curriculum for special learners.

I met this new author, Jo Grace, when I recently funded part of her online 'Kickstarter project' based on sensory stories, from which she launched her mission to write this book. It is a substantial book which pulls together many different sensory strands, weaving them into a rich tapestry of sensory story creations. It also offers a sensory approach reflected in the relevant anecdotal stories, notes and ideas of the writer, woven into each chapter.

Sensory stories for very special children and young people have developed over the last few years to become significant creative factors in their education and learning. This has evolved from the work of significant ' hands on' writers such as Keith Park, Melanie Nind, Pete Wells, Nicola Grove, Sheree Vickers and Andrea Muir to name a few as well as the charity Bag Books. It has also been taken up in major dramas reflected in theatre production groups such as Bamboozle, Oily Cart and Head2Head.

They all delight in pushing special learners from concrete sensory stimulation into spontaneous and creative communications and fun. Jo's book joins this elite group.

When we dip into this book there are various significant strands, on a variety of different levels, to follow and explore.

The strands include:

- Sensory stimulation and learning dominates every life, cradle to grave, without exception. For special people it is the same but sensory stimulation should be a dominating and exciting feature of daily life and living.

- Sensory stories offer a powerful voice of communication. The participants can have a strong voice, either active or passive, so long as the reader listens and positively reacts to their voice.

- 'Including everyone' is a fundamental human belief and sensory storytelling has no barriers.

- Sensory stories, ideas and resources usually have a base of concrete materials. These carefully selected sensory items arouse curiosity and exploration during the storytelling. Jo emphasises that these materials should cost little or can be begged or borrowed. There is no need for expensive purchases. There is a need for imagination and forays into charity shops seeking them!

- On a research level, there is strong strand linking Jo's ideas to academic evidence within the book, gathered from significant educational research, writing and events.

I trust this book will reach and touch many readers, inspiring them to use sensory stories as a key to unlocking excitement, fun and enjoyment for every listener.

Flo Longhorn, Principal Consultant in Special Education and Author

INTRODUCTION

What is a sensory story?

A sensory story is a story told using a combination of words and sensory experiences. The words and the experiences are of equal value when conveying the narrative. We know that sensory experiences are important and carry meaning: our instinctive interactions with infants are often in the form of sensory exchanges, and old adages such as 'a picture speaks a thousand words' and 'actions speak louder than words' testify to our knowledge that sensory stimuli convey meaning. Modern research, which will be discussed within this book, continues to provide further insight into the value of sharing stories in a sensory way.

Sensory stories were originally developed for individuals with profound and multiple learning disabilities (PMLD) by people such as Keith Park and Nicola Grove and organisations such as Bag Books and PAMIS. They are a simple, engaging, fun resource, which can be used with a wide range of learners and enjoyed by everyone. Part II of this book will give you ideas of how you can use sensory stories with different learners.

How I discovered sensory stories

I began my teaching career at a school for students with severe and profound special needs. My class had a wide range of abilities and included a child with PMLD. I was also expected to teach in the segregated PMLD class. I had a lot to learn. I was keen to do well and enthusiastically prepared lessons at the weekends and during school holidays that I hoped would work, but after delivering these lessons I was always left with a sense of having let the students with PMLD down. My teaching assistants were great and made sure everyone was involved in whatever task I had set, but I could read their faces and see they were thinking, 'Are you sure this is a good idea?' I was out of my depth and I was failing to communicate with all my students equally, and then another teacher in the school suggested I try a sensory story.

Sensory stories enabled me to teach my whole class; more than that, sharing sensory stories with the children with PMLD felt meaningful and I could clearly see that they were responding. By using sensory stories I was able to facilitate learning at a level appropriate to all my students, including those with PMLD.

I was the religious education coordinator for the school. During my summer holiday following my discovery of sensory stories I created a set of sensory stories based on narratives from different faith traditions. Each story was kept in a large cardboard box. I remember the caretaker's face as he wondered with dismay where we were going to store them in our already cramped school. I learned a lot creating those first stories. I got funny looks in shops as I hunted for something that would feel just like an elephant's tusk. I struggled to choose the essential bits of the narratives to form the text. I made decisions about style and content, and the worth of particular stimuli. Further down the line, the school bought in sensory stories from outside (which saved me from spending another holiday on the hunt for peculiar items), and through using those stories, as well as my own, I gained insight into what worked and what did not work for my students. I developed a better understanding of how to make a really great sensory story and thoroughly enjoyed creating stories to support the curriculum for my class.

Since leaving the classroom I have had the opportunity to read the research underpinning sensory learning. It was reassuring to discover that many of the things I had stumbled upon whilst teaching are backed up by the research. I wanted sensory stories to be available to everyone and not just to people time-rich enough to spend weeks puzzling over what would make a particular noise or people with deep enough pockets to be able to afford pre-resourced stories. In 2013 I took the opportunity to launch the Sensory Story Project, which aimed to create five resource-yourself affordable sensory stories. Thanks to numerous backers the Sensory Story Project was a success: the stories were created, and this book is one of many wonderful things that have happened as a result of the project.

About this book

The following chapters introduce the importance of sensory stimulation and the significance of narrative. The role that narrative has to play in the inclusion of individuals with special educational needs and disabilities is considered. We look at the benefits to be gained from combining sensory stimulation and narrative together. Along the way we also look at: the senses we have (our famous five, plus two extras); what makes for strong sensory stimuli; and how it is possible for a short text to convey a whole story.

Part II of this book focuses on how to share sensory stories with a wide range of learners, including those with PMLD, sensory processing disorder, autism spectrum disorder, attention deficit hyperactivity disorder, sensory and physical impairments, mental health difficulties and memory difficulties. Guidance is provided on ways to tell the stories to maximise their learning benefits.

Part III contains suggestions for how to use sensory stories as the basis of interactive sessions with individuals of all ages and abilities, including adults and individuals with no additional needs. Part IV deals with assessment, beginning with why you might want to undertake it and ending with a few methods you might like to try.

Part V of this book contains five new sensory stories. Each story comes with a set of activities and lesson plans to help you make the most of the learning opportunities it provides. These are not just for teachers; anyone planning to tell the stories on more than one occasion will find something useful here.

More information can be found on my website http://jo.element42.org.

I hope you will find this book an enjoyable, easy and useful read. Have fun creating and sharing sensory stories.

PART I

Background

1

THE IMPORTANCE OF SENSORY STIMULATION

Sensory stimulation is central to our cognitive development (Ayer 1998). It is not just useful or an added extra; it is necessary. When a child is born, it is the information received through its senses that wires its brain (Bruner 1959; Gabbard and Rodrigues 2007; Piaget 1952).

One easy way to think about early cognitive development is to consider the brain as a densely overgrown forest. When we have a sensory experience it sends an electronic pulse through our mind, creating a neural trace. If this experience is repeated, the trace becomes a pathway. Think of the experience as a person walking through it, they wouldn't make much of an impact, but as they walk more, the pathway would become well worn.

Experiences from different senses form different pathways through the forest. At a point where two pathways intersect, coordination develops between our senses. When sight coordinates with touch (or proprioception) we develop hand-eye coordination. The development of hand-eye coordination is not possible without first experiencing a wide range of sensory stimuli. Many important developmental milestones follow from the development of hand-eye coordination.

Sensory stimulation is not only necessary for brain development, it is also necessary for the maintenance of our faculties (Bruner 1959). In the forest of the mind, if a well-trodden path were no longer walked it would grow over and become lost. Most of us lead lives in which we will never experience the sort of sensory deprivation that could cause the loss of our abilities. However, some people may have to live in environments that are low in sensory stimulation; other people may purposefully avoid sensory stimulation (Chapter 5 on sensory processing disorder will explain more about why they may do this); other people's access to sensory stimulation may be limited by their physical abilities.

Early on in my career I attended a Richard Hirstwood training session. Training aimed specifically at people who worked in special schools was very hard to come by, particularly in rural Cornwall, so I was very excited to find such a relevant course. Richard told a story that serves as a very stark illustration of the 'use it or lose it' aspect to our sensory abilities. At the time I did not see it as a story so much as a test, here is what happened:

It was the start of the day. I was in a room full of people who did similar work to me. Many had been in their roles for 20–30 years; I had been in my job for just two years. I was very nervous. Richard welcomed us and explained that the first thing he wanted to do was tell us about a man he had worked with and we were then to diagnose this gentleman. I was alarmed; I thought that Richard was testing us to see how knowledgeable we were before he continued with the day. I knew I didn't stand a chance at guessing the condition of someone I hadn't met.

The man Richard described had a hunched-over body position and limited movement of his limbs. He could walk but not very far. He did not respond to visual or auditory stimuli and did not speak. His eyes, ears and vocal cords had been tested, and as far as the medical profession knew there was nothing physically wrong with them. I had no idea what condition was being described, however, a few more-senior members of the group put their hands up and guessed at rare conditions that I had never heard of. They were wrong. That the experts got it wrong gave other people the courage to venture answers. The guesses got progressively more vague, 'Was it some type of this, or a sort of that?' people wondered aloud. Richard kept up a steady stream of 'noes' in response.

Finally Richard told us what had happened to the man. When he was 17 he had broken up with his girlfriend and as a consequence had become very depressed, not getting out of bed in the morning and crying constantly. His parents were so distressed by his state that they had him committed to a local asylum. There he was put into bed by staff each evening and in the morning he was got up and sat in a chair beside the bed. Each day this was repeated: bed in the evening; chair in the morning. Bed-chair, bed-chair, bed-chair. This cycle was maintained for 15 years.

The man's body was the shape of the chair he had sat in for those 15 years. It was not that he had become blind but that he had become personally disconnected from his sense of sight. He had no interest in seeing anymore: he'd seen the same view for 15 years. The same applied to his hearing. His needs had always been met. He'd had no reason to communicate. Without reason or cause to use his senses or his abilities he had gradually shut down and withdrawn entirely into an inward world.

We are all so accustomed to living sensorially rich lives that it is easy for us to overlook the need for sensory stimulation – to think of it as a fun activity and nothing more. Sensory stimulation is vital for our development and vital for a happy life.

Sensory stimulation and children with physical or sensory impairments

We instinctively know the importance of sensory stimulation to the developing child; we dangle bright objects above babies, make silly noises, give them tactile toys to grab and chew. All of these things are great for promoting their cognitive development, but we should not underestimate just how much sensory stimulation a developing child accesses independently.

Imagine a typically developing child lying in their cot: the child hears a noise and turns their head to see what made the sound; the child spots a splodge of colour and reaches out with a hand to investigate what it might be. A typically developing child engages pretty much constantly in this sort of activity. All of these small investigations help to develop neural pathways in their mind.

Now imagine a child with profound physical disabilities lying in a cot; the child hears a noise but cannot turn their head; the child sees a shape but cannot reach out to investigate further.

Researchers investigating different aspects of provision for individuals with disabilities all comment on the diagnostic overshadowing which can occur (e.g. Hayes *et al.* 2011). It is very easy for people to believe that the cognitive delay observed in children with profound and multiple learning disabilities is a direct result of their disability, and not question whether it is a consequence of their not having had as much stimulation as typically developing peers. Yet if we look to the research that talks about early cognitive development and the importance of sensory stimulation, we find a wealth of researchers talking about how important the environment and the stimulation within it is to development (e.g. Glenn 1987; Gray and Chasey 2006; Hayes *et al.* 2011; Lacey 2009; Longhorn 1988; Vlaskamp *et al.* 2007; Ware 2003, cited in Gray and Chasey 2006). Ayer (1998, p.89) stressed the importance of sensory stimulation to development by saying, with reference to the development of hand-eye coordination: 'The child with profound and multiple learning disabilities, combined with sensory and physical impairments, requires a sensory curriculum in order to bring them to this important stage of intellectual and motor development'.

The child who is unable to access sensory stimulation on their own begins their development on the back foot. It is very important that carers seek to provide individuals with profound disabilities with a wide range of sensory experiences. Sensory stories are one way of offering such stimulation.

The inability to access sensory stimulation independently does not only affect a child's neurological development; it also affects their attitude towards learning and engagement with life. Researchers found that some of the perceived passivity observed in individuals with profound and multiple learning disabilities was not solely down to their disabilities, as had previously been assumed, but was a form of learned helplessness. Hayes *et al.* (2011) report individuals with profound intellectual disabilities as suffering with low mood, making them less likely to engage in activities. They also found low mood could be the cause of negative behaviours displayed by individuals with conditions such as autism spectrum disorder, and speculated that antidepressants could be a more effective treatment than the currently prescribed tranquilisers.

Reflecting on the new-born child in their cot, it is easy to see how this could occur. The child lies in their cot, hears a sound and wants to turn their head to see what made the noise, but cannot. The child sees a shape and wants to reach out for it, but cannot. The child is interested in the world, curious about it, keen to engage with it, but learns over and over again that it is out of reach. It is natural that they would eventually give up trying to find out about it. Children unable to access the world around them can turn inwards for stimulation, and become disengaged with the world. This limits their ability to learn and their desire to communicate. In extreme cases individuals will self-harm in order to get the stimulation they desire.[1]

Sensory stories are one way of providing individuals with a range of sensory experiences.

Our senses – the famous five, plus two

We have five famous senses and a few others that not everyone has heard about. The five famous ones are touch, taste, hearing, smell and sight. I have seen up to 18 additional senses added to this list, but for the purpose of this book I will be adding just two more: our vestibular sense and our proprioceptive sense. We use these senses to help us to understand where our body is and what is happening to us.

---

1   It is important to note that self-harm in individuals with PMLD can also indicate that they are feeling pain.

Your vestibular sense relates to balance and movement. Picture yourself in a completely closed-in, sound-insulated lift. You know when it starts to move. You have not used your sense of sight, because it is completely closed in. You did not use your ability to hear, because it is sound insulated so you are not able to hear the motor start. You did not use taste or smell, and the only touch you experienced was your feet against the floor. It is your vestibular sense that tells you that the lift is moving.

Your proprioceptive sense tells you where your body is in space. Try this experiment: put a cup on a table then turn around and reach behind you with your hand to pick up the cup. My bet is that you are able to do this with relative ease. I expect that you reached straight for the cup – you did not look, you certainly could not hear where the cup was, nor did you sniff or taste your way there. You might have felt your way along the edge of the table, but I doubt it; I expect you were able to reach straight for the cup. You were able to reach for the cup without looking because you knew where it was and you knew where your body was in space; that is your proprioceptive sense in action.

As with your other senses, your vestibular and proprioceptive senses can be impaired. A person may have stronger or weaker proprioception. Individuals with low proprioceptive sense will seek to discover where their body is through their other senses; this counters the unnerving sensation of not quite knowing where their bodies are. Someone with low proprioception may well fidget a lot because this will give them feedback through their sense of touch about where they are. Similarly, tipping and spinning can be ways of amplifying the information received by the brain from the vestibular sense.

Teachers and parents may view a child who is engaged in something like fidgeting or spinning as being distracted from their learning. I am not saying every child who tips their chair or fidgets has a sensory impairment, but I can say that it is possible that these sorts of behaviours may actually help, rather than hinder, a child's concentration.

A person in a state of anxiety is not in an optimal state for learning. Fear activates our primitive fight or flight response, which actually bypasses the part of the brain responsible for learning. A frightened child will not learn. A child who feels anxious because they are unsure where their body is will look to soothe that anxiety in some way. If they are able to soothe their anxiety then they will be in a state ready to learn. As teachers and parents, it is our job to find ways to provide for children's needs in a manner that suits their environment; for example, a child who seeks feedback about where their body is by tipping their chair can be given an elastic physio band (or a pair of tights) to wrap around the legs of their chair; they can then press against this band with their feet and get the feedback they need without distracting other learners. Other children respond well to being given small toys to fiddle with whilst they listen, or feel less anxious when wearing compression clothing.

What makes for strong sensory stimuli?

Sensory stories are told using words and sensory stimuli. Unlike a picture book, the stimuli are not merely an accompaniment to the words; they are as much the story as the words are, so just as we choose the right words for a story, we should also choose the right stimuli for a story.

When picking sensory stimuli to tell a story I think about two things: how great an experience does the stimulus give, and how connected is the stimulus to the story I want to tell? To tell a good sensory story you need to get both these things right. It is no good having a great set of sensory stimuli that have nothing whatsoever to do with the narrative bending the narrative to fit the stimuli you happen to have, having a great story that is told through a weak selection of sensory stimuli.

A strong sensory stimulus is one that wholly engages a sense, or one that demands attention from a sense. Children's books are often illustrated with pictures. A picture is not a strong visual experience by itself. To be interested in a picture you need prior knowledge about what a picture does, an understanding that pictures convey information and represent life, and to be interested in what might be in that picture. Without this understanding, a picture is just a selection of coloured blobs in a particular location.

Imagine a teacher reading a picture book in front of the class. The teacher presents the children with a page of colours and lines. On the classroom walls behind the teacher are colourful posters, to the side are the children's coats and bags of different colours and textures and on the tables are colourful pencil tins. The children have no reason to look at the picture in terms of its visual features alone.

A strong visual experience could be something that impacts your whole vision. It need not be complicated – looking through a sheet of coloured cellophane changes *everything* you see; it is a big visual experience. The absence of light – for example, experiencing total darkness from a blindfold – is another big visual experience. Things with high contrast, for example, bright lights against dark backgrounds or an indoor sparkler, will also naturally draw the eye and be strong visual experiences. Moving items may also draw the eye more strongly than static objects, as the sensors in our eyes that pick up on movement are different to those that record colour and shape. Some individuals may find it easier to perceive a moving object than a static one.

Once you start to question experiences in this way it becomes easier to discern what makes a strong sensory stimulus. A strong touch experience does not have to be experienced with the whole body, although a whole-body experience, such as being submerged in water, would certainly be very strong, if a little difficult to facilitate within the context of a story. I encourage you to try touch experiences out and see what makes you pay attention. Think about where a touch experience happens; we do not have to touch with our hands. The skin on our forearms or the soles of our feet is very sensitive – touch experiences are stronger if delivered to sensitive locations on the body. How we experience touch can also affect its relevance to a story. Consider a story about a trip to the beach; would feeling sand between your toes be a more pertinent experience than sand on your hands? A favourite touch experience of mine is to create a teardrop using a small pipette or a drinking straw and dropping the tear onto a person's face on the cheek exactly where a tear that had been cried would fall. That feeling of a tear trickling down your face is a very particular feeling. The skin on your cheek by your nose is very sensitive. It is an experience you notice and pay attention to, which makes it a strong experience in itself. If used to tell the part of a story where someone is crying, the connection to that part of the story is a strong experience, because that *is* what a tear feels like as it runs down your face.

It is good to be creative when thinking about touch experiences. Too often I have seen cuddly toys used as touch experiences – does a toy lion really offer a similar touch experience to a wild lion? I have seen swatches of fabric used to represent a character's clothing, and I am left wondering whether this was an important part of the story. To be interested in what the character's clothes feel like, first I have to know there is a character, and to understand anything about that character from touching their clothes, I have to understand the significance of silks, lace and gold embellishments and so on. It depends on the fabric, but many will not make for strong touch experiences because we so commonly touch fabric in daily life. I expect today you woke up touching the fabric of a sheet and blanket and maybe your nightwear, you then got up and touched a range of other fabrics as you put on your socks, underwear and clothes. You may also have touched tea towels, bandages, nappies, coats, scarves, cuddly toys, curtains, bags and so on throughout the day. My guess is that if your hand brushed against a piece of fabric you would not stop to see what it was, however, if you put your hand in something sticky, you would stop and look, want to know what it was and even shriek and pull away. A good touch experience will grab your attention; a really great one will not only grab your attention but also be relevant to the story and make you want to explore it further.

What makes for a strong sensory experience is personal to each individual. In the above paragraph I gave an account of a life where fabric was commonplace, but suppose I was a child growing up in poverty – in a mud hut in a slum, without clothing. I am more likely to have touched a plastic bag than a piece of velvet. To that child, touching a swatch of satin or fur fabric would be a big experience. When choosing sensory stimuli for a story we need to be aware of our own sensory experiences of the world and also of the experiences of the person with whom we intend to share the story. Recently I have begun collaborating with a speech and language therapist who supports individuals with dementia. Together we have been thinking of strong sensory experiences for her clients; slowly we are developing a list of things that link to the world they remember from their youth: the whistle of a kettle on the hob, an air raid siren, mint humbugs, sherbet dips, carbolic soap and so on. Sensory experiences are personal to each person and influenced by their abilities, experiences, preferences, life and the times they live in.

Sound and taste experiences are usually easier to discern in storytelling, as they tend to be the items from the story. For example, in a story where someone eats a sandwich, you can eat a sandwich. In a story where a drummer plays, you can play a drum. Sound and taste are also two senses we typically pay more attention to. We know what we like and do not like to eat; we can become passionate about flavours, returning to a restaurant for a particular sauce or begging a friend for a particular recipe. We have favourite songs and bands, and we know how our emotions are swayed by different sorts of music. Through our experience of sound and taste we enrich our lives; a pleasurable taste or sound experience is a luxury to us – a treat, something we value – so most people have a pretty good idea of what makes for strong sensory experiences in regards to these senses.

Taste does not have to be an experience only for those who are able to chew and swallow. Many individuals with PMLD spend some time being tube fed and cannot take food orally. A taste experience can still be provided by touching a flavour to the tongue. Pineapple juice is said to stimulate more taste buds than any other flavour; a drip of it on the tongue could be a rich taste experience. Some experiences lie on the boundary between taste and touch; consider an ice cube held against the lips or a metal spoon in the mouth – both could be thought of as taste experiences. Today you can buy many different flavours of lip balm, which can also be used as taste experiences where actual food is not appropriate.

Smell is generally a pretty overlooked sense, yet people in old age often remark on how certain aromas take them back to a particular time in their life. For me, the smell of Stickle Bricks will always take me back to my first primary school classroom. If I asked you what you smelt yesterday you would probably struggle to remember unless something significant had happened to you. Thinking about what smells you remember can provide clues as to what would make a great smell experience. Of course, particularly pungent smells come high up the list – if you stepped in dog poo yesterday you would remember the smell but that sort of smell can be difficult to share safely with someone in the context of a story so keep thinking. Perhaps you smelt a loved one's perfume? Perhaps it was the smell of something fantastic cooking?

Thinking about what would make a good stimulus for the proprioceptive or vestibular sense can be tricky, as our awareness of these senses is new. Movement can be used to address both of these senses, and touch experiences often combine to form proprioceptive experiences as well. As with all of the senses, by simply paying attention to our own experiences in everyday life we develop our insight into what makes a strong experience in the context of a sensory story.

2

THE SIGNIFICANCE OF NARRATIVE

The word 'story' conjures up pictures in our mind of childhood storybooks and sweet tales told to young children to get them to sleep at night. Stories are not just relics of childhood; they permeate our lives and contribute to forming our identities. There are the stories we tell each other about what we did at the weekend, whether our team won or lost and what he or she said at work the other day. There are the stories we share from our history, culture or faith group. There are the stories we've been told about who we were when we were little. There are the stories we share in together through films, TV and books. Stories enrich all our lives.

The ability to form our experiences into a story helps us to hold onto and remember them. Stories help us to share our experiences and interest others in our lives. In sharing a story we seek out and receive acknowledgement that our lives are interesting and worth living. We interest others in us and draw others close to us, furnishing our lives with friendships, which are necessary for such social animals as ourselves.

Through listening to other people's stories we learn things about life without having to experience them ourselves, just as stories with morals in them teach us right from wrong. Listening to other people's stories allows us to think about what we would have done in the situation they describe. Stories let us decide who we will be and design our own identities. Many people will hold characters from stories up as heroes or models for their life, striving to emulate aspects of those characters in their own life.

The telling of a story, and sharing in that telling, is a bonding social event. This is true of all sorts of stories, from those read from the pulpits of churches, uniting the parishioners in a shared set of beliefs, to those told in pubs, on buses or at home. Joining in with these stories, whether it is by saying 'Amen' or by laughing along at the appropriate points, is our way of saying, 'I am part of this,' and 'I am with you in this life, we are not alone.' Not to be included or able to join in is to be isolated and alienated in the extreme.

Families will tell stories of events they all shared in: remember that Christmas when Grandma sat on the cat? These shared reminiscences and 'in' jokes bond us and form part of our identity. We are told stories about who we were when we were little – these shape our notion of self. We share in stories from our culture, history and time. Some sound more worthy than others, but all have their part to play; for example, I am in my mid-30s and I know if I meet someone else in their mid-30s and I quote a line from the TV series *Friends*, they are likely to know what I am on about. We will have something in common; we will feel a connection, just through sharing in a story. The person who cannot share in these common stories misses out on being able to form connections with others in this way.

I have a small personal insight into what it is like to be the one left out of these stories. When I was a child I lived on a boat. I watched dolphins leaping over the boat's bow waves and played on deserted beaches. It was a wonderful childhood. We settled on land around the time I started school. The boat did not have a TV and neither did our new house. I did not notice the absence of TV until I was in the playground. Gaggles of girls would circle the playground inviting people to play games with them. I was invited to play Ewoks – I had no idea what an ewok was, so I could not play. Other games offered were: She-Ra, The A-Team and Muppet Babies – all equally puzzling to me. The girls wanted to include me but they could not because I did not share in those stories with them; when I tried to engage them in conversation about beaches and dolphins they did not understand.

To be left out of stories is to be left out of a part of life. When we seek to include individuals with special educational needs and disabilities in life, inclusion in stories should be a part of that, not only in sharing stories but also as characters.

Gwendolen Benjamin contributed the narrative to 'The Forest of Thorns' story which appears in Part V of this book. Here, Gwen talks in her own words about the links between stories and society:

> Stories are in a constant dialogue with society. Each generation is shaped by the stories of those that came before, and then goes on to tell their own stories. Secondary socialisation is the process by which we learn norms and values from the society in which we are raised. This includes the stories we read or are told. Any stories we create will be unavoidably influenced by our norms and values. This can take an insidious form. The term 'The Smurfette Principle' was coined in 1991 by writer Katha Pollitt who noted that too often, a single female character is included in an ensemble cast, solely playing the role of the

token girl. This reinforces the idea that male is the default gender and women take a secondary role. A similar effect can be seen in the ratio of white to non-white characters in Western media. A sole instance of this in a story may not cause a problem, but when we are exposed to the same idea over and over it can become normalised. As I writer I try to be hyper aware of any messages my work may be conveying, because I am aware of the power they can have. While stories can be an immense power for good, they can also be damaging.

We can see how stories and society are entertained by looking at the way world events affect what stories are told. I am a huge nerd, so I love *Star Trek*. When the original series first aired in 1966 the cold war was in full swing and this is reflected all over the stories. The most obvious example is the Federation's tense relationship with the major villains: the Klingon Empire. Mysterious, militarised and clearly dangerous opponents, the Klingons embody a stereotypical view of life behind the iron curtain. As the cold war petered out and the franchise continued, their portrayal becomes more nuanced and sympathetic. Early in 2013 the film *Star Trek Into Darkness* was released. One of the driving events of the film is a terrorist attack and the reactions to it, reflecting life in a post-9/11 world.

Stories reacting to shared traumatic events are nothing new. Noah's Ark can be taken as an example: God floods the entire world, tasking Noah with rescuing animals so life may continue. Stories of a global flood can be found in many cultures, including one of the oldest surviving stories: the Epic of Gilgamesh. It is likely that these are a response to a large-scale flood, or a number of them, that really happened. Stories about such events serve as a record of them, but they are also a safe space to deal with them. Putting something in a fictional context can remove the real-life baggage that surrounds it, making it easier to re-examine.

Gwen is beginning to touch upon what researchers have termed 'the storytelling space'. This space in which stories are told and shared has been found to have special properties. In the storytelling space we are braver, we feel more confident and we are better able to cope with life's challenges. In the storytelling space we are omniscient and unafraid, we understand things better than we do in real life and we can face things we fear. Jo Empson's book *Rabbityness* (2012) is a good example of the way this special space can be utilitised. *Rabbityness* is a beautiful book in which one rabbit dies and the other rabbits mourn him by finding ways to remember him that make them happy. I have used this book many times to talk to children about how to respond to bereavement. Children who would not know how to talk about the death of their grandfather, pet or friend find in *Rabbityness* a way of telling me about what their loved one was like and quickly come up with things their loved one enjoyed doing.

Sharing in stories makes our lives richer and bonds us together. To share stories with individuals in a way that is meaningful to them is to include them in life and to offer them the opportunity to benefit from all the wonderful things narrative has to offer us. Sharing sensory stories is one way of doing this.

Why combine sensory stimulation and storytelling?

Sensory storytelling provides both the opportunity to deliver richly stimulating sensory experiences to an individual and to share a story with them. The story aspect adds a structure to the sensory stimulation, and this structure can be further reinforced by maintaining the sort of consistency explained in Chapter 3 of this book. Having a clear structure means that experiences can be repeated. Repeating experiences increases their predictability to the individual experiencing them, and this in turn increases feelings of security that the individual will feel in relation to the experiences. Repetition is important for learning to occur. Presenting experiences in a structured way enables the development of memory and anticipation (Gray and Chasey 2006).

Sensory stimulation is valuable in itself; I am not advocating that all sensory activities should be structured. We should aim to present all learners with a range of activities, regardless of their abilities. When we consider the lessons that take place in a typical primary school, some will be more structured than others. Some learners will flourish where there is structure and others will flourish where lessons are relatively free flowing. If we present only unstructured, or only structured activities to our learners, we limit their opportunities.

What can you say in ten sentences?

Sensory stories are usually pretty short. The stories in this book are all under ten phrases, and the content of each phrase is intentionally concise. Researcher Penny Lacey writing in *PMLD Link* (2006) said that sensory stories *are* literacy for individuals with PMLD. Penny is highlighting that sensory stories are not a substitute for the real thing; they can be the real thing. Engaging in sensory storytelling is a valuable literacy activity for individuals with PMLD, not a substitute for literacy. Literature covers a rich and broad range of writings, from poetry to fairy tales, sci-fi to chic lit, historical fiction to literary fiction. I hope that one day sensory stories will span as broad a range.

It might seem improbable that different genres of writing could all be created within so few sentences, but it is possible.

As part of the Sensory Story Project I worked with a physicist to create a sensory story about the birth of stars in stellar nurseries. In seven sentences we were able to explain all the essential facts involved in the creation of stars and convey them in a way that formed an interesting and engaging narrative. We created a very concise piece of non-fiction. Another Sensory Story Project story was told in the form of a haiku; it is a piece of poetry. Within this book you will find a story based on folklore, another that can be sung, a sci-fi adventure and more. You will find stories suitable to story experiencers of all ages. Gwen's story is based on the traditional fairy tale of 'Sleeping Beauty' and is written in the fantasy realism style, so that is another two genres ticked off the list. We're getting there, and we're not the only ones: PAMIS (which stands for Promoting A More Inclusive Society) is a Scottish charity that has created stories based around what are seen to be as sensitive topics, such as personal hygiene; Bag Books is a UK charity that creates resourced sensory stories that tell fun children's stories about trips out or magical adventures.

I hope in future to witness a continued expansion in the stories that are available to individuals with PMLD.

PART II

Sharing Sensory Stories

3

HOW TO SHARE A SENSORY STORY

Telling a sensory story is very simple; first you need to gather all the sensory stimuli you will need for the story. Having a box designated to the story to keep your stimuli in is a great idea. To share the story you simply read each line and facilitate the accompanying experience. It may be that the experience is delivered at the end of the sentence or it might be delivered during the sentence, for example, on the particular word that relates to that stimuli. That is all there is to it!

Maintaining consistency when sharing sensory stories

How you go about sharing a sensory story will depend very much on whom you are sharing it with. For some individuals, having a sensory story shared with them in a consistent manner can help them to develop their understanding, communication and expression of preferences and also relieve them of any anxieties they may feel around sharing the story and so enable them to interact with the stimuli more.

Sharing a sensory story in a consistent manner is still simply a case of reading the words and facilitating the stimuli; it's just that with consistent telling you will be aiming to read the words and facilitate the stimuli in the same way each time you deliver the story.[2]

Here are a few of examples of why you might want to consider consistent sensory storytelling.

---

2   A short film (four minutes) on maintaining consistency is available to watch here: www.youtube. com/watch?v=reBMH0ODr2s.

Example 1: Expressing preferences

I am telling a sensory story that involves two different smells. I make sure I deliver the smells in the same way each time I tell the story. The person I am sharing the story with always seems more interested in the floral scent than the citrus scent.

Their behaviour communicates to me a preference for the floral scent. My close observation of their reaction to this stimulus allows me to 'hear' them expressing that preference. I can use that information in the future on their behalf, for example, if I were to go shopping to buy them shower gel, I'd look for one with a floral scent.

If each time I had told the story I had delivered the scents in different ways – perhaps making a big fuss out of one and holding it close to the person whilst just offering the other for a moment, or on some tellings presenting the citrus scent in a prolonged and steady way but waving the floral scent back and forth beneath the person's nose – I wouldn't know if their preference was for the scent or for the way I had delivered it.

Of course, this depends hugely on who is experiencing the story with you. You may be telling the story to someone who could tell you each time, 'I like this smell best.' For that individual, varying how you deliver the experience might be a way to keep the story interesting. The correct way to tell the story always depends on you and the person with whom you are sharing the story.

Example 2: Demonstrating learning

I am telling a sensory story that involves a loud noise. The sentence that precedes this noise is, 'She heard a bang.' I plan to tell this story every day for a week.

On Monday I say, 'She heard a bang.' I make the sound. My story experiencer flinches at the sound and then laughs with enjoyment. I observe their flinch reaction and consider that it could count at around P level 1, which requires individuals to show a reaction of any kind – flinching included (for more information on the P levels see pages 76–82).

On Tuesday I say, 'She heard a bang.' I make the sound. My story experiencer flinches at the sound and then laughs with enjoyment. I observe that their reaction is consistent with Monday's reaction and begin to wonder if P level 2 might be more fitting. At P level 2 individuals are becoming consistent in their reactions to stimuli.

On Wednesday I say, 'She heard a bang.' I make the sound. My story experiencer flinches at the sound and then laughs with enjoyment. I am happy that P2 is fitting.

On Thursday things happen just as they did on Monday, Tuesday and Wednesday, but on Friday something really interesting happens.

On Friday I say, 'She heard a bang' and my story experiencer begins to laugh before I have made the sound and their body tenses ready to flinch. I make the sound. They flinch and continue laughing. This pre-emptive response communicates to me that they knew what was going to happen next. That was their way of saying, 'I know what happens next in this story and I like it; this bit is my favourite bit of this story.' They have demonstrated anticipation, which is a skill that maybe evident in individuals operating at P level 3.

Being able to put a number to someone's achievements is not important; you are not telling the story as some kind of test or simply to be able to fill in data sheets, but being able to demonstrate that an individual is capable of learning (and to use numbers to do that) is a great weapon in the fight for inclusion and can have a ripple effect on how they are viewed by the people around them.

Now consider a different version of events…

On Monday I say, 'She heard a bang.' I make the sound. My story experiencer flinches and then laughs with enjoyment. I think, 'Oh they like this bit!'

On Tuesday I say, 'She heard a bang.' I make the sound several times. My story experiencer flinches and laughs and laughs. I am thrilled with how much they are enjoying it.

On Wednesday I am looking forward to this part of the story, I say, 'Ready? Here comes the good bit. She…heard…a…BANG!' I make the sound several times. My story experiencer flinches and laughs.

On Thursday I am not able to tell the story so I ask someone else to tell it on my behalf. They say, 'She heard a bang,' but they are worried about the noise that the stimulus might make so instead they pass it to the story experiencer to hold. The story experiencer does not react.

On Friday I am able to tell the story and am looking forward to it. I say, 'She heard a bang,' and go to make the sound but cannot find the stimulus as the person from the day before has put it away in a different place. Eventually I find it and make the noise. The story experiencer flinches and laughs.

In this second version of events the story experiencer has had a stimulating time. Chapter 1 on the importance of sensory stimulation showed that these experiences are valuable in themselves, but in this version of events the story experiencer has not been enabled to communicate their understanding of the story.

Consistency can be a very useful tool in sensory storytelling. If you are aiming for a high level of consistency then think about how you will achieve this. If it is likely that someone else will be telling the story as well can you develop a system whereby you share in detail what you do and what responses you have observed? I am not recommending that *all* sensory experiences should be this consistently conducted – that would make for a very rigid and dull life. This is *one* way of providing a learning experience and there are many others.

Tips for consistent sharing of sensory stories

- Be prepared.

- Take your time.

- Stick to the text.

- Know the person with whom you are sharing the story.

Being prepared

Telling a sensory story involves reading set sentences and facilitating sensory stimuli. In some situations you will be taking it in turns between the reading and the facilitating; in others you will be facilitating as you read. To be able to do this smoothly you need to have all your sensory stimuli laid out somewhere easy to reach. Stopping to find a particular stimulus, or work out how to switch it on, will interrupt the flow of the story.

It is also a good idea to prepare yourself for reading a sensory story by reading it through out loud on your own first. This will give you a feel for how the words sound when you say them. We are all different and have different turns of phrase; if you feel a particular sentence does not work for you, or you will struggle to pronounce a particular word, change it beforehand rather than adapting on the hoof. If someone else is going to be sharing the same sensory story with the same individual then it can be a good idea to do this preparation together to ensure you will both be saying the same thing.

Once you have your wording and your stimuli organised think about how you will deliver them. Will a particular word be spoken loudly? Will you be facilitating a touch experience to someone's left or right side? Will a sight experience be presented up close or far away? There are lots of things to think about. It helps to know the person you plan to share the story with well so that you can facilitate the stimuli, and speak, in a way that best suits them.

Taking your time

You may be able to rattle through the sentences and deliver the stimuli in just a few minutes, but this will not give the person you are sharing the story with a chance to absorb and respond to what is going on. I can best illustrate this point by drawing on an example from another communication strategy that is often used with individuals with PMLD: communication switches.

A communication switch is a large, easy-to-press button that can record a short message. Individuals with PMLD can learn to press these switches; the hope is that the recorded voice can speak words that individual would say if they could. It is a great idea, but its success depends very much on how it is carried out. Here is an example from a classroom:

> The teacher is delivering the register, calling each child's name in turn. Each child replies, 'Good morning.' When the teacher gets to the child with PMLD the teaching assistant places a switch, upon which is recorded 'good morning' on their lap tray. The child does not respond, so the teaching assistant lifts the child's arm and places their hand upon the switch, whereupon the switch says, 'Good morning,' and the teacher continues with the register.

This physical assistance to operate the switch is not in itself bad practice. The child with PMLD will need to have the experience of pressing the switch a few times before they begin to understand what it does. Physical assistance teaches them that when they move their arm and place their hand on the switch, the switch says, 'Good morning.' However, the physical assistance continues beyond the child learning this, communication is being squashed rather than facilitated.

Think about what is going on inside the child as they hear their name called in the register. At first their brain must recognise that it is their name. They must then remember that they are expected to respond with, 'Good morning.' Once this is recalled, the brain must remember how to go about saying, 'Good morning.' Messages must be sent to the arm and to the hand to move. The arm and hand must act on these messages to move and finally the switch will be pressed and will speak 'Good morning' on behalf of that child. All of this processing takes a long time and whilst it is going on the child seems to be doing nothing at all.

We are used to a flow of speech that is very brisk, and many people feel uncomfortable in long silences. If the child is given the time they need to respond then they are enabled to communicate. If someone lifts their hand and does it for them, they are prevented from communicating.

When we are facilitating sensory experiences within sensory stories we need to allow for this same processing time. A touch experience placed in the hand and then whisked away again might not be noticed. Someone who appears at first to not be responding may just be processing all the information they are receiving. Learn to feel comfortable in the pauses. Teach yourself to stay present with the person and the story (you may be in character) during these pauses. Watch the person with whom you are sharing the story closely for signs of response. For some people these signs will be obvious: big body movements or loud vocalisations; for others they may be far more subtle: a change in eye gaze or a relaxing of a small facial muscle. If you know the person well and watch them closely over time you will become accustomed to spotting their responses. Someone who is able to 'listen' to such subtle responses makes a great communication partner for an individual with PMLD.

Sticking to the text

Sticking to the text of the story means that your words become auditory cues for the sensory stimuli, enabling the person with whom you are sharing the story to know what is coming next. Consider again the example of a teacher calling the register (page 39). The child in the example knew that when their name was called they were to say, 'Good morning.' Now suppose some days the teacher does not use names but simply says, 'Good morning' to each child in turn whilst looking at them and on other days uses their surnames instead of their first names. In a situation where the auditory cue changes it is harder for the child to learn the expected response.

Keeping to the wording of the story sounds so easy to do, but it is easy to add in auditory padding or verbal prompting, for example, when offering a smell experience: 'Mmm doesn't that smell nice, can you smell that? Mmm, isn't it lovely?' or when offering a touch experience: 'Here, it's here, touch it with your hand, that's right, like this, can you feel it?' These verbal extras are often produced without thinking. They come naturally to us as people used to the speedy to and fro of conversation and aware of the awkwardness most people feel in silence. For individuals who struggle with verbal communication a flurry of words can be confusing, can make it hard to pick out the important keyword and can overwhelm. This is not just a point to consider when sharing stories with someone who may need longer than average to process information; it is also one to bear in mind when sharing stories with someone who may find language difficult. Individuals with autism spectrum disorder or attention deficit hyperactivity disorder (ADHD) will often struggle to process language, so providing less language may make an experience more enjoyable for them. Once again, the right choice is all down to the individual you are sharing the story with.

Choose what you will be saying ahead of sharing the story with someone, and stick to the text you have decided on. Feel comfortable in the silences; share them happily with your story experiencer and remain in the story as you do so. Think of other ways to offer any prompting that might be needed, for example, gently guiding a person's hands towards a touch experience on the first telling of a story. Overall, hold back from what radio DJs would call 'filling'.

Knowing the person with whom you are sharing the story

When sharing sensory stimuli with someone it is important to have some background knowledge on their sensory abilities, preferences and allergies. Clearly it is important not to give people taste experiences to which they are allergic. It also makes sense to facilitate a sound experience to the left ear of an individual who is deaf in their right ear. Knowing about people's sensory preferences can support you in facilitating the story in a more sympathetic way, for example, if you know someone jumps easily at loud noises, you need not make the loud noise in a story at full volume.

It is quite easy for us to think we know a person well, but we may not realise what knowledge we are missing: you do not know what you do not know! This truism was exemplified by Vlaskamp and Cuppen-Fonteine's study (2007) – staff who supported adults with PMLD in a care home were observed offering their clients the choice of whether to listen to music. This choice was offered by placing a music tape in front of the person – if they picked it up this was taken to mean they wanted to listen to music. If they did not pick up the tape staff took it to mean that they did not want to listen to music. The researchers found that in some situations the tape was being placed in a location where it was difficult for the person to see it. There are many variations in people's sight: some people will find it easier to see close up; others far off; some will be able to see moving objects but not static ones; people can have tunnel vision or impaired tunnel vision, only seeing things that are straight ahead of them or on the periphery of their vision. Try using the assessment on pages 83 and 84, which is based on Vlaskamp and Cuppen-Fonteine's work to see how well you know your story experiencer.

4

PMLD, LABELLING AND THE ROLE SENSORY STORIES HAVE TO PLAY IN INCLUSION

The term 'PMLD' used to indicate profound and multiple learning disabilities is inconsistently applied across the literature surrounding special educational needs and disabilities. Applying labels to individuals is an innately flawed system, but labels are a way of communicating. Basic nouns are labels that allow us to communicate about groups of objects. When we use labels to denote groups of people we have to hope that anyone listening understands that within the denoted group there will be a great deal of variation. Everyone is unique and labels should not be used to hide that. I will attempt to define the group I mean to denote when I use the term 'PMLD'.

An individual with profound and multiple learning disabilities will typically have profound physical disabilities as well as severe cognitive impairment. It is likely that they will have sensory impairments and experience seizure activity.

Individuals with PMLD are often thought to be the most profoundly disabled members of our society, and expectations about what they are able to do or achieve can lag behind our expectations of individuals with other learning disabilities. Sadly it is not very long ago that individuals with PMLD were thought to be incapable of learning. I have often been asked during my career whether I consider their lives to be worth living. This is a shocking question, however, it was not asked by callous people, but by people seeking to understand something. It is a question I have never been asked with respect to other learning disabilities.

Practice has come a long way since the days when we locked people in institutions and threw away the key; however, it has not come far enough. In some schools and care settings out-dated practices and beliefs are still being exercised.

Sensory stories have a role to play in changing how people with PMLD are viewed. If I am able to use a sensory story to show someone that an individual with PMLD can learn, can communicate and has opinions about things, I know that this will change the way they treat that individual. The demonstration of learning – the fresh understanding of what constitutes communication – has a lasting impact. In terms of advocacy, I think sensory stories are worth sharing as a way of demonstrating someone's abilities as well as for the developmental benefits they offer to that individual.

I have another reason I enjoy sharing sensory stories with individuals with PMLD: I love being the person who gets to communicate with them. Not because there is anything more special about them than anyone else, but because not everyone gets to do it. For me, the opportunity to be one of the people who gets to communicate with a group of people so many others miss out on communicating with, is exciting. However, this motivation is one I am happy to relinquish. I look forward to a day when everyone feels at ease communicating with individuals with PMLD and it is a normal occurrence, not the thrilling one I currently find it to be.

I believe that reactions to individuals with disabilities that might at first glance appear to be prejudice may actually be people who are afraid of getting things wrong. I have worked with teachers who worried about teaching individuals with PMLD in case they (the teachers) inadvertently said something wrong. In PMLD Link (Anonymous 2006) a letter writer asks how they should break the ice when meeting someone with PMLD. The person writing this letter may appear stand-off-ish in regards to their behaviour towards individuals with PMLD, whilst on the inside they want to meet and chat. Parker (2011) describes a scenario in which a non-disabled child wishes to make friends with a disabled child but does not know how to go about making the first moves. Her writing is based on multiple students that she has observed over her career. Sensory stories have a facilitating role to play: people feel more confident taking part in an activity they are familiar with; we all know how to tell stories. Being invited to share a story with someone can give people who are otherwise a little daunted by the prospect of interacting with someone with a disability the support they need to make that first step.

Matthew Clark (Raphael and Clark 2011, p.18) makes a very important point about communication with individuals with PMLD. He writes about Christian Raphael, a young man with PMLD whom he supports. Matthew points out that many people view Christian as not being very good at communicating because of his physical limitations. Matthew sees Christian in a different light: 'Christian is a skilled communicator who utilizes that which is available to him in a consistently effective manner.' The ability of someone with PMLD to communicate is as much to do with our listening skills as it is to do with their expressive communication skills.

Sharing sensory stories with individuals with PMLD

Telling sensory stories consistently, using the tips from Chapter 3, will provide someone with PMLD not only with a fun and stimulating range of sensory experiences, but also with the opportunity to communicate and demonstrate their learning. The tips are all simple to implement, but, ironically, they are as easy to get wrong as they are to get right. Research by ten Brug *et al.* (2012) found that after a day's training 84 per cent of those trained were able to create sensory stories according to guidelines given by PAMIS, but only 1.3 per cent went on to tell those stories correctly. It is easy to make sure you have all your sensory stimuli in easy reach before you begin to tell a story (tip 1) but just as easy to forget to check the battery on your torch. It is easy to take your time over telling a story (tip 2) but just as easy to rush to get it told before a TV programme starts. It is easy to read the sentences as they are written in the story (tip 3) but just as easy to add in extra comments of your own. Chapter 3 should have given you a good understanding of why these simple tips are worth following when sharing a story with someone with PMLD. Of course, the very idea of there being a right and a wrong way to share a story between two individuals is a funny one; I hope that having read this book you will be able to find a way to share sensory stories that is right for you and right for the person with whom you are sharing them.

A number of the benefits offered by sensory stories to individuals with PMLD have already been covered in Chapter 3 – the opportunity to: communicate; express preferences; demonstrate learning; take part in storytelling; bond within the storytelling space. There is one final benefit I want to mention before this section closes, and that is the possibility of building someone's confidence in the world.

Confidence in the world

Individuals with profound disabilities are vulnerable in the world and rely on the care of others. It is natural that someone with profound disabilities will find unfamiliar circumstances or experiences distressing. If they are not helped to overcome this distress they can end up leading lives where their access to new sensory experiences is limited. Sharing a range of sensory experiences within the safety of the storytelling space – in a location where the individual feels secure and in a predictable and consistent manner – can help people to become accustomed to new experiences.

Imagine the following scenario:

I am walking along the seafront with a friend who has PMLD. My friend is enjoying the smell of the sea and feeling the warmth of the sun upon their face as I wheel them along.

Suddenly a dog barks. My friend is frightened – this is a very natural, sensible response to a loud animal sound. The set of experiences my friend is going through have become alarming and our walk is no longer a pleasant experience but is now a distressing one.

If my friend had encountered the sounds of a dogs barking within the context of a sensory story, in an environment where they felt safe and secure, then they would recognise the sound and perhaps not be alarmed. Our walk could continue to be an enjoyable experience.

Experiencing a range of sensory stimuli within the security of a sensory story can support a person with PMLD to build their confidence at encountering new stimuli and open up the world to them.

5

SENSORY PROCESSING DISORDER

Sensory processing disorder (SPD) has only recently become recognised as a condition in its own right. Previously SPD was *viewed* as an aspect of conditions such as autism spectrum disorder and ADHD with which it commonly co-occurs, but scientists have begun to find evidence, such as differences in the brain structure of those with the condition, which suggests that SPD can occur on its own (Owens *et al.* 2013). Research in this area is still in its infancy; there is much left to find out and learn.

An individual who has SPD will struggle to handle the information their brain receives from their senses. This difficulty with the processing of sensory information can manifest itself in different ways. The following explanation is based on Dunn's model of sensory processing (Dunn 1997, 2007), which I find particularly clear.

Individuals with SPD have different neurological thresholds to individuals without the disorder; this means that normal levels of sensory input (i.e. the kind of sensory stimulus one could commonly expect to find in everyday life) are either too much for them or not enough. If everyday sensory stimulation is too much for a person then they may find the day-to-day world overwhelming; such an individual would be considered to have a low neurological threshold. If everyday sensory stimulation is not enough for a person then they may find the day-to-day world terribly dull and uninteresting; they would be considered to have a high neurological threshold.

People can react to these differences in neurological thresholds actively or passively. Someone who reacts actively will seek to do something about the imbalance they feel – either by blocking out stimuli they find too much or seeking to create stimulation where they do not feel they are getting enough. Someone who reacts passively will experience their difference as a form of discomfort but will not try to do anything about it.

This combination of high/low neurological thresholds and active/passive responses produces four different manifestations of SPD.

High neurological threshold – passive response
Someone with a high neurological threshold who responds in a passive way will appear bored, aloof and disengaged with the world around them.

Low neurological threshold – passive response
Someone with a low neurological threshold who responds in a passive way will seem uncomfortable, distracted and slightly distressed.

High neurological threshold – active response
Someone with a high neurological threshold and an active response will seek to find sensory stimulation in their environment; people can be very creative in how they go about doing this. I have known children to empty bathroom products completely and smear them around (lots of smell and touch experiences). Responses like this, although catastrophic to a tidy home, can be quite funny, however, children may also self-harm or harm others to gain stimulation, which can cause a great deal of distress.

Low neurological threshold – active response
Someone with a low neurological threshold and an active response will seek to block out the stimulation they find overwhelming. Strategies such as closing eyes, turning away and blocking ears can all be utilised to block out stimulation. Some people find they cannot tolerate the feel of clothing against their skin and so remove it or select particular clothing, for example, items without seams. In extreme cases individuals may turn to self-harm, for example, hitting their ears or hitting their heads, in an attempt to shut everything out.

Individuals with an active response to their sensory processing difficulties tend to be easier to spot than individuals with passive responses. It is good to be mindful when working children (and indeed adults) that sensory processing may play a role in behaviour. Although it is not easy to spot the passive responders, if you have an awareness of SPD you may be able to spot changes in an individual's responses based on location; for example, I once met a child who only talked when it was dark. That child's mother felt that whilst it was light the child felt too overwhelmed to speak, but in darkness, with the associated lack of visual stimulation, they were able to relax and communicate. I have also seen secondary school students thought to be low achievers come alive with interest and insight when a text was presented to them in a sensory way.

SPD and sensory stories

Individuals with SPD benefit from sharing sensory stories in two ways that are specific to the disorder, as well as in the other ways discussed in this book.

1. Sensory stories can give them the opportunity to encounter and get used to stimuli.

2. Sensory stories can present them with the opportunity to practise their responses to stimuli.

Individuals with SPD can struggle with eating difficulties, and sensory stories have a role to play in supporting people in addressing these difficulties.

The following three sections discuss these benefits in more detail. If you are sharing sensory stories with an individual with SPD, you may also find that many of the tips for consistent storytelling in Chapter 3 will be useful.

Sensory stories as a way of introducing, and becoming accustomed to, stimuli

It is natural for us to be wary of new experiences. We do not know whether they are safe and our instinctual caution protects us from spontaneously tasting that funny coloured mushroom or reaching into the brightly flickering flame. We are all a little bit anxious of encountering new sensory experiences: how do you feel about touching that slug or holding that spider? What about tasting an oyster for the first time or sniffing stinky tofu? It is also natural for us to find some sensory experiences overwhelming: music that is just too loud, the sound of fingers down a chalkboard, etc.

Nature has ways of letting us know that new experiences are safe. If we see someone else have an experience and nothing bad happens, we begin to think we might be okay to have the same experience. We know we should try a little bit of something first and wait to see if anything bad happens before trying more. We are able to educate our palates to like tastes we initially disliked; this is a process of learning that the taste is safe. Many coffee drinkers will know that when they first tasted coffee they found it bitter and unpleasant, but once they had learned to like the flavour they never looked back. We can create a similar progression of experiences for someone encountering sensory stimuli in the context of a sensory story.

For individuals with SPD the opportunity to regularly encounter new sensory stimuli through repeated telling of a sensory story can afford them the opportunity to grow accustomed to those stimuli and not feel overwhelmed by them. Some stimuli may even come to be enjoyed.

Using a sensory story to facilitate these encounters is beneficial, as the story element wraps the process up in fun whilst also providing reassurance about what is going to happen next. Once the story is familiar it will feel safe, and the lack of surprises will be relaxing and enjoyable.

Regular exposure to a range of sensory stimulation can help individuals with high neurological thresholds to 'retune' their sensory systems so that they are more receptive to the stimulation found in daily life.

Your approach when sharing a sensory story with an individual with sensory processing difficulties who has a low neurological threshold will very much depend upon that individual and what they are willing to experience and can tolerate. You will need to decide how many new experiences to allow in a story and how best to facilitate those experiences.

You can present a chosen new sensory experience in the same way on each retelling of the story. The benefit of this is it becomes very predictable and the person experiencing the story knows exactly what is going to happen. You would, in this instance, be looking for more interaction with the stimuli from the story experiencer on each subsequent telling of the story. For the story to be successful, the individual with SPD needs to find it a safe and enjoyable place, so avoid putting too much pressure on them to interact with stimuli. A little prompting or encouragement may be necessary; perhaps you can share the story with two people at once and have the second person really enjoy the interactions with the stimuli as a way of tempting the individual with SPD to have a go. We are bolder and braver within the storytelling context, so your timid story experiencer might surprise you.

A second option is to grade the stimuli that you are expecting the story experiencer to interact with; this could also be done in reverse for individuals with high neurological thresholds. In the case of an individual with a low neurological threshold, you might begin by not expecting them to interact with the stimuli at all but merely watch someone else's interaction. In subsequent tellings of the story, you would be looking for them to interact with a weakened version of the stimuli. Over future tellings, you would gradually increase the stimuli until the final telling has the individual experiencing the stimuli at full strength. For a story experiencer with a high neurological threshold, you could begin with an exaggerated version of the stimuli and over retellings dilute it down to a subtler stimulus.

Sensory stories as a way to rehearse responses to stimuli

We should not expect everyone to be able to cope with every sensory experience – no one has this expected of them in life. Personally I find music in nightclubs too loud, mushrooms too slippery and dog poo too smelly; I do not expect these sensory preferences to change. It is unrealistic to think that through practice an individual with SPD will be able to master every sensory experience they encounter.

If you believe that your story experiencer is not going to be able to learn to tolerate an experience then you have a decision to make: is it an experience they must have? Ask yourself: is it an experience that they will come across in life? Would avoiding that experience impact negatively on their life? If it is an experience that is a necessary part of a balanced life then your aim is to teach them how to deal with and respond to the experience when it happens. If it is an experience that can be avoided without damaging their life then your aim is to teach them appropriate ways of avoiding it.

We all have sensory experiences we dislike; knowing how to avoid them or how to respond appropriately are important skills to learn. Here are a couple of examples.

Fingers down a chalkboard

Imagine that the first time I hear this sound I am a baby – the noise upsets me and so I scream and cry. The next time I encounter this sound I have reached my terrible twos – this time I shout and hit the person making the noise. I get a little older and a little wiser and when I next hear the sound I am able to put my fingers in my ears and block it out. A little older and a little wiser still with a few extra social skills and next time I encounter the sound I am able to ask the person making it whether they could please stop as I find the noise unpleasant. You can see in this example that there is a progression to my responses. What this progression is depends upon the stimulus. The opportunity for me to encounter a stimulus within the context of a sensory story on repeated occasions gives me the chance to practise more sophisticated reactions to that stimulus.

Mushrooms

I dislike the taste of mushrooms and I can avoid them. I make choices in restaurants that do not involve mushrooms; I pick them out of my food (when no one is looking); I choose not to buy them in the shops. These things might limit my life experiences a little and they might be a little impolite, but they are not going to significantly impact my life. I have learned to cope with my dislike of mushrooms. If I hadn't managed to acquire these coping strategies, the opportunity to encounter mushrooms within the safety of a story and not be required to eat them, but instead be given strategies to inform my reactions, would be very valuable to me.

In some cases we may be able to teach individuals with SPD strategies for avoiding stimuli they cannot tolerate (like showing me how to pick mushrooms out of my food). In other cases we may be looking to teach them ways of coping with the unpleasantness of having those experiences (like showing me how to put my fingers in my ears in response to an unpleasant sound).

Sensory stories can be a first step in identifying experiences that individuals find hard to cope with. They can also provide a place to practise reactions to stimuli where getting it wrong will not be as catastrophic as in real life. It can help to make story experiencers aware of their reactions. Talking about a reaction can help the story experiencer become self-aware and manage their responses. Recording reactions on each telling of a story can help story experiencers feel a sense of progress. Even if progress is made in very small steps, having a record can help – you can point to small changes and express your expectation that more changes will occur, as well as your confidence in them to be able to make those changes (a recording method like those illustrated on page 88 and pages 90 and 91 would suit this process). Together you can pick a goal to work towards, for example, 'I will see a mushroom without screaming.' Setting such a goal and recording the steps taken to reach it will help the story experiencer to feel that it is going to happen.

Some sensory experiences are necessary for life – necessary for our survival (such as eating). When an individual with sensory processing difficulties struggles with a necessary life experience it can be very distressing for them and their loved ones. Sensory stories provide a simple way of helping people with SPD to encounter and cope with a wide range of sensory experiences.

The role of sensory stories in addressing eating difficulties

Eating is a very sensory-rich experience. If you find eating overwhelming and distressing, this is going to impact your life in a negative way. Learning to avoid eating is not an option; the only option is a gradual process of desensitisation.[3]

The most important thing when supporting a person with a difficulty like this is to maintain a low-pressure environment. Addressing the difficulty at a time that is not a mealtime, in a context different to mealtimes, is a good first step. Try to identify which aspect of eating that the individual is struggling with. Is it the smell of the food? Is it the consistency or texture? You may be able to answer these questions by observing their reactions to other sensory stimuli they encounter during sensory storytelling sessions. They might be happy touching sticky substances but resistant to smelling strong smells. Building up a picture of an individual's sensory preferences is instrumental in helping them to progress and develop.

Once you have identified the specifics of the problem, you can begin to address it. If you cannot identify a specific problem and believe all aspects of eating to be challenging then you can address them one by one. Take eating as a touch experience as an example: young infants often lift objects to their

---

3   It is important to recognise that eating difficulties can be caused by many different things. If someone you love is struggling to eat, ensure they get the right medical attention to find out the cause of the difficulty.

mouths to touch them; this is because the lips and tongue are very sensitive to touch and so they are able to get detailed information about an object by touching it with their mouths. If you are someone who struggles with touch then touching with your mouth is going to be very difficult. You can start by getting used to touching things with your hands or even feet. Offering food substances to be touched and explored without the pressure of having to eat them gives a person the chance to build up familiarity with what they are feeling. Once they are able to touch something with their hands they can begin to try touching it with their mouths. You may have to begin with non-food substances – do not worry; just gradually increase the diversity of textures encountered and work towards touching food.

There is no one solution; progression will be specific to each individual and their particular abilities and struggles. You can also play with eliminating senses from the equation, for example, by blindfolding a story experiencer as they experience the story or by placing a diving peg on their nose to block their sense of smell. It is possible that you will find that an approach like this makes the very sensory experience of eating a little bit less sensory and so a little bit less overwhelming and more manageable. In the long run you may be able to find subtler solutions, like choosing foods that do not have strong odours or wearing dark glasses whilst eating.

The most important thing, and equally the hardest thing to do, is to allow the sensory journey to be one without pressure. Just share the story and enjoy it. Allow progress to happen naturally, however slowly that might be. Once you feel progress has been made you can begin to make the transition between story and real-life application – a starting step could be to tell the story at the dinner table (not at dinner time); another step could be to start telling stories about food, for example, the 'Seasoned with Spice' story in this book.

6

❊❊❊❊❊❊❊❊❊❊❊❊❊❊❊❊❊❊❊❊❊❊❊❊❊❊❊❊❊❊❊❊❊❊❊❊

SENSORY STORIES AND...

Sensory stories are great for sharing with anyone, as the added sensory stimulus supports engagement and memory. When I deliver training days on sensory stories I always tell a sensory story and a non-sensory story to the delegates. People find it easier to remember the sensory story; they find it more interesting.

I could present an endless list of different conditions for which sensory stories have relevance, but that would make for rather a dull read. I have opted to select a few conditions and highlight the specific benefits sensory stories hold for individuals with these conditions. It is by no means an exhaustive list; I hope that reading this book will provide people with the knowledge and insight they need to discern whether the stories hold any specific benefits for the people they know.

Sensory stories can be widely differentiated, making them ideal to share with individuals with a wide range of needs and abilities. In Chapter 7 I outline three key ways sensory stories support learning and development for individuals with special educational needs and disabilities.

...individuals with autism spectrum disorder (ASD)

Individuals with ASD can find verbal communication difficult. The sparseness of the language within a sensory story can make the information conveyed by that story easier for an individual with ASD to take on-board. When someone does not understand an idea or a concept our tendency is to explain more – to add language until we have explained the concept in as many ways as possible. This verbal approach to understanding can be difficult for an individual with ASD to contend with. In a sensory story the stimuli act as an explanation and can help an individual with stimulus understand what is being conveyed by the story.

SPD often co-occurs with ASD. Recently I met a leading ASD researcher at a conference who told me confidentially that they believed the sensory processing aspect of ASD was responsible for many of the traits we think of as being typical of ASD. It was their belief that an individual with ASD spends so much of their cognitive capacity coping with their sensory environment that very little is left over for other endeavours, such as communicating and socialising.

Imagine that an individual's total cognitive capacity – that is, all the space they have in their brain for thinking – is represented by the large square as in Figure 6.1. The small square inside the left-hand large square represents how much space is taken up in the average mind by processing sensory information. You can see there is a lot of space left over for other activities. The large square in Figure 6.1 represents what the mind of someone with ASD might be like. If more space is taken up by processing sensory information then there is less space left over for other tasks. I like this visual representation. You could also think of the smaller squares as the space taken up in the mind by processing language or coping with anxiety. Both squares represent people who are coping with their experience; if the inner squares were to eclipse the outer squares that would represent someone who was not coping, or who was having a 'meltdown'.

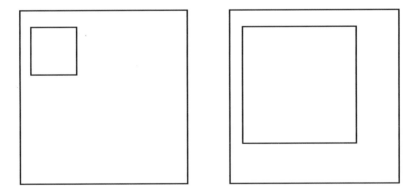

Figure 6.1 A representation of cognitive capacity

Individuals with ASD may benefit from the opportunity to encounter and become accustomed to sensory stimuli presented by sensory stories in the same way as individuals with SPD. Individuals with ASD may find information conveyed in a concise way, as happens within sensory stories, easier to take in than language-rich information. Most people find concepts explained through sensory media easier to understand than those explained with language alone, for example, in my sensory story, The Birth of a Star, gas is described as spinning. The word spinning is accompanied by a visual experience of something spinning. It is much easier to understand what the word spinning means when you are watching something spin. For individuals who struggle with processing language, as can happen for individuals with ASD, the non-verbal explanation provided by sensory stimuli can support understanding.

The section on inspiring interaction in Chapter 7 (see page 61) may hold particular relevance for those wishing to share sensory stories with individuals with ASD.

...individuals with attention deficit hyperactivity disorder (ADHD)

Individuals with ADHD can struggle to concentrate. I have had students explain to me, 'I can't concentrate, I have ADHD,' as well as teaching assistants and parents saying the same thing about individuals with ADHD. ADHD does not mean that you are not able to concentrate, but it does mean that it is likely to be harder for you to learn the skill of concentrating.

For those of us who find concentrating relatively straightforward, it can be easy for us to view concentration as having just a few components, for example, as you read this book you are concentrating because you are looking at the page and reading the words. In a classroom a child might be considered to be concentrating because they are looking at the teacher and not talking. In actual fact these identifying characteristics of a concentrating person are only the last few steps of a series of skills that have to be mastered along the road to concentration. I expect as you read this book you are sitting on a chair; perhaps you've been sitting for quite some time. One of the skills you have is the ability to sit still in one place – to tolerate what how it feels as the circulation in your body adjusts to that sitting – perhaps your bum has gone numb. You can imagine that a child sitting cross-legged on a classroom carpet has to contend with the feeling of their ankle bones pressing into the floor; they also have to ward off other sensory distractions, for example, noises outside the classroom, pictures on the wall and the fidgeting of other children. If you are not initially able to concentrate then you move, and you do not get the chance to develop those underlying skills, for example, the ability to sit still.

We know that some things are easier to concentrate on than others. If I were to stand before you and lecture you for two hours in a monotone, you would find it hard to concentrate, whether or not my lecture is interesting. However, if I sit you in a cinema and ask you to concentrate for two hours I bet you would find it easy.

Sensory stories offer individuals with ADHD something to hang their concentration on – they have something to listen to, touch, smell and so on. It is easier for them to sit and listen to a sensory story than it is for them to listen to a typical story. That experience of concentrating gives them the opportunity to practise all the skills involved in concentration. It is not that they must always have information presented in such a stimulating way, but that by presenting information in a way that makes it easy for them to concentrate you are giving them the opportunity to develop the underlying skills of concentration that they can draw on later in less stimulating situations.

SPD often co-occurs with ADHD and so Chapter 5 on sharing sensory stories with individuals with SPD is worth reading.

…individuals with sensory impairments

If one or more of your senses does not function properly then having access to information via your other senses is very important. It is a mistake to think that sensory stories will not be suitable for someone who is, for example, blind or deaf because they involve sight experiences or sound experiences. If someone is completely blind then sight experiences will need to be substituted with an alternative experience – a story such as 'Seasoned with Spice' would be ideal for sharing with a blind individual. There is always scope for swapping experiences to make a story more relevant to a particular experiencer. Total impairment of a sense is relatively rare – many people will have a partial impairment – so related sensory experience may still be appropriate. A strong sight experience may suit someone with a sight impairment, as it will be a visual experience they can access.

The broad range of experiences presented by sensory stories mean there is a wide palette of experiences for individuals with sensory impairments to access. When I am asked about the possibility of using sensory stories with individuals with sensory impairments I often think about an experience I had early on in my teaching career.

> My school allowed me to observe various outside practitioners who came into the school to work with our students so that I could learn from what they did. I remember watching a young man who was totally blind reading to a specialist Braille practitioner in a 1:1 session. His task was to read the Braille on the page and also to extract information from the accompanying tactile picture. This picture was an exact replica of the picture in the book, but made out of vacuum formed plastic so that what were lines in the book were ridges in the plastic and colours in the book were textures in the plastic. The picture was of a child playing on

a swing. The young man read the Braille text successfully and answered questions on it with enthusiasm. He was then asked to identify which piece of playground equipment the child in the story was playing on. This information was only available in the picture. He half-heartedly put his hand on the plastic and then shrugged and said, 'I dunno.'

The touch experience of a piece of bumpy plastic is not a great one; it feels much the same as the plastic wrapping on toys or the lid of one's packed lunchbox – it was not an interesting touch for him. This particular young man had been blind from birth; the lines representing the swing meant nothing to him as they represented a visual world. Had he lost his sight then the lines might have meant something to him. In his world a swing is the feel of the rope or chain that holds it up, the movement of the seat and the feel of the wind on his face. I hope that if he had been reading a sensory story on the same topic, the accompanying touch experience would have been an engaging one for him.

...individuals with communication difficulties

Individuals who find verbal communication difficult for whatever reason – a stutter, nerves, an enlarged tongue or other physical difference, etc. – need lots of practice at verbalising. However, many individuals who experience difficulties in enunciating words become self-conscious about trying to speak and end up speaking less, not more, than normal. Extra support to be understood can give an individual with speech difficulties the boost of confidence they need in order to have a go at verbalising. As with the above example, signs and symbols can help, as can sensory stimuli. Consider a story with the words 'bright blue light' within it. An individual with a speech impediment may pronounce this as 'ight ooo ight'. If they are asked simply to speak the words they may be hesitant to do so, knowing that 'ight ooo ight' will be hard for others to understand. However, if they are to facilitate the stimulus of a bright blue light as they say 'ight ooo ight' they will have added confidence in their being understood. Using the stimulus to support their communication means that the individual is more likely to be understood when they speak and so get the encouraging feedback of being understood, which will give them more confidence to try verbalising again in the future.

Sensory stimuli can also be used by individuals with communication difficulties to answer questions about stories without having to verbalise at all. Learning needs to be accessible to all and should not be contingent on a person's particular disability. Teachers will naturally want all their students to be able to speak confidently and clearly. We would never make learning contingent upon one's ability to walk; we should not make it contingent upon people being able to speak. Taking part in sensory stories allows individuals to build an understanding of the turn-taking nature of communication. Using sensory stimuli, students can answer questions about a story, such as, 'What comes next?' and 'Which was your favourite part?' They can demonstrate their recall of the story by facilitating the stimuli in the correct order. Having an alternative means to communicate gives people the chance to learn communication and literacy skills independently of mastering the skill of language.

…individuals with memory difficulties

When we learn in a multi-sensory way, more of our brain is engaged in learning. For someone with memory difficulties, having more of the brain engaged in a task gives them more chance of being able to remember the task. It also gives them more avenues to their memory. For example, if I had read you a typical story called *Starshine* in which a boy goes on an adventure to the stars, I might ask you about it the following day. I might ask you if you remember the story by using its name, 'Do you remember *Starshine*?' I might try describing what happens, 'Do you remember the boy going on a journey?' and so on. Although I am approaching the memory in different ways, I am actually only giving you one sort of prompt: a verbal one. If I had read you The Birth of a Star I could ask if you remembered it by name, but I could also ask through repeating one of the stimuli to see if you appeared to recognise the experience.

Sensory stories provide information in a multi-sensory way; when repeated in a consistent way they can be easier for individuals with memory difficulties to remember than typical stories. The sensory stimulation within the stories supports the creation of memories.

…individuals with physical impairments

Chapter 1 dealt with the importance of sensory stimulation, explaining that sensory stimulation is vital for cognitive development and for engagement in life. If an individual has a physical impairment that limits their ability to access stimulation for themselves then providing them with extra stimulation through the use of sensory stories can be very beneficial (see Chapter 1 page 21).

…individuals with mental health difficulties

Individuals with mental health difficulties can seek to withdraw from the world. Life can become overwhelming for them and human contact too much to cope with. In this respect they can be very similar to someone with SPD who has a low neurological threshold. Gently exploring a sensory story with an individual with mental health difficulties can encourage them to re-engage with life.

Sensory stimuli can be very emotive, for example, particular smells may bring back strong memories, or particular touches may be comforting. When sharing a sensory story with an individual with mental health difficulties, allow space for them to explore their emotional response to the stimuli.

Chapter 3 explains how to share a sensory story in a consistent manner. It may be that if an individual with mental health difficulties is feeling particularly vulnerable, the familiarity and predictability brought about by consistent repetition of a story will be soothing. However, sticking rigidly to consistent telling could prevent spontaneous sharing of responses or exploring of stimuli, so you might be looking to begin by telling the story consistently but on later retellings pull back from this consistency and allow your story experiencer to take more of a lead role and explore their personal responses to the story.

7

SUPPORTING LEARNING
AND DEVELOPMENT

Understanding vocabulary

Individuals with special educational needs can find language tricky to understand. Individuals with ADHD or ASD can struggle to hold the words in a sentence in order and to pick out the important ones. Individuals with a learning disability, or people attempting to communicate in a language that is not their mother tongue, may struggle to understand the meaning of words. There are many conditions and situations that can impact a person's ability to understand language. Supporting language by another means helps people to identify the important parts of spoken language and understand their meaning. Systems such as Makaton and Picture Exchange Communication are ideal for doing this: keywords are identified and displayed as signs or symbols, giving listeners an extra way to understand what is being said. Sensory stimuli can play a similar role. Consider a story containing the sentence, 'It was hot.' Hot is the keyword in this sentence. A picture of someone sweating on a midsummer's day would give second-hand information about what the word hot means, but touching something hot gives direct experience of the meaning. Sensory stories can directly support individuals in understanding vocabulary.

Concentration, learning and memory

The added stimulation provided by the sensory aspect of sensory stories makes them easier for people to concentrate on, which enables them to practise the skills involved in concentration; this is discussed in detail in the section on ADHD (see Chapter 6 page 55).

A person's ability to concentrate has a clear impact on their ability to learn; as concentration improves so learning opportunities increase. Sensory stimulation further supports learning as it aids memory (see page 58).

Inspiring interaction

Communication can be a very daunting experience for some individuals with special educational needs and disabilities. The concentration of information and intensity of social contact that is involved in standard communication can be overwhelming. It is natural for individuals to avoid situations that feel overwhelming to them; being forced to take part only serves to exacerbate the anxiety they feel. Sensory stories can be used to encourage, even tempt, people into communicating. The use of sensory stimuli to convey meaning within a sensory story means that there is less pressure on the text to convey everything. The smaller word count of a sensory story when compared with a typical story may mean that people who find spoken communication difficult will find a sensory story easier to engage with.

A proactive way of using sensory stories to engage people in communication is to make them a desirable experience or the object of curiosity. Here is a technique you might like to try.

1. Store the sensory stimuli needed for your story in a fabulous-looking box; if you are creative, make one.

2. Arrange a situation whereby you, the box and the person you hope to engage in communication are all in the same place, ideally somewhere relatively bland so that the box is the most interesting thing.

3. Have in mind a particular set of conditions, relevant to the individual with whom you will be sharing the story, that you want fulfilled in order for the story to be told. You might want the person to sit down; you might want them to make eye contact with you or to look at the box; you may simply want them to be looking towards you. The conditions you come up with teach the individual about what is involved in communication. If you are happy to share a sensory story with someone who is simultaneously watching TV or climbing on furniture then you are saying that to do these things whilst communicating with someone else is okay. You do not have to formulate conditions that exactly represent standard communication straight away; you can build them up over time. At first you might look for them simply to look towards what is happening but not come near, or you may want them to stop vocalising in order to let you speak but be happy for them to roam around whilst you speak. Later on you might look for more from them.

4. Sit in a relaxed fashion yourself and look interested in the box; you could even peak inside. You are aiming to excite their curiosity about what is in the box.

5. When your personalised conditions are met, open the box and begin sharing the story.

6. Stop sharing the story as soon as your conditions are no longer being met.

7. Restart if the conditions are met. (Imagine you have a 'pause' button.)

This stopping and starting enables the person with whom you wish to communicate to control how much communication they experience. Having control over the situation will lessen their anxiety about taking part. Over time you can build up your expectations and they can build up their ability to tolerate. In this way you can both enjoy sharing the story together.

PART III

Using Sensory Stories to Form the Basis of Group Sessions

8

STRUCTURING SESSIONS TO CHALLENGE AND INCLUDE A RANGE OF LEARNERS

In an ideal world you will be able to share a sensory story 1:1 with your story experiencer. However, very few of us operate in an ideal world. Sensory stories can be used as a structure to build learning experiences around; using the stories in this way can enable you to include a range of learners in a shared experience.

Bookending

Sensory stories have very few words but a lot of content. The content of sensory stories can be expanded upon to challenge a range of learners. Take the story 'Seasoned with Spice' as an example. 'Seasoned with Spice' is about cooking; learners could be expected to:

- experience cooking facilitated by someone else

- help out with cooking in small ways, for example, by stirring a mixture

- follow a basic recipe themselves

- comment on an item as it's being cooked

- compare two recipes and pick the best

- design their own recipe

- create a recipe to serve a particular purpose, for example, a healthy cake recipe.

These activities cover a wide range of achievement, but they are all about cooking and all directly relate to the story.

Bookending a session with a sensory story involves telling the story at the beginning and the end of the session and providing activities at a level appropriate to your learners in between. This is the structure used for all the lesson plans in this book and you will notice that the activities in subsequent lessons are ordered according to the story, with the activities in earlier lessons relating to the start of the story, and activities in later lessons relating to the end of the story. There are many benefits to this structure, which are outlined below.

Bookending sessions with a sensory story can support the mind in organising the information gained within those sessions. Knowing where information is stored in the mind helps us to retrieve that information in future, for example, if you ask me to multiply seven by nine I know you are asking me a maths question and mentally I reach for the parts of my brain that deal with maths. Language is the primary way information is organised within the mind. Our minds undergo structural changes when we acquire language, almost as if they are big filing cabinets, and language enables us to label the pockets within them. For individuals who have not yet acquired language sensory stimuli can be used to organisation information; for those who have acquired language sensory stimuli can reinforce that organisation.

Sharing a sensory story at the start of a session is a good way of introducing a topic and providing an overview of where that session's learning sits.

Sharing the sensory story at the end of a session allows individuals time to reflect upon their learning and fit it into the context of the bigger picture supplied by the sensory story.

Repeating the story over time is likely to result in individuals memorising the story. The story can then be used as an aide-memoire for all the learning that took place within the sessions bookended by the story.

Building

You can build up a sensory story over a series of sessions with individuals. In session one you might share only the first couple of sentences of the story, allow your story experiencers to experience the associated sensory stimuli and then complete a learning task based on those sentences. At the end of the session you would revisit those sentences. You can choose between asking story experiencers to predict what might come next in the story or sharing the next few lines as a preview of the following session.

Building has many of the benefits of bookending; the main difference is that individuals do not hear the full story until the final sessions in the series meaning that it will be slightly harder for them to memorise the whole story.

However, not telling the whole story all at once allows for people to predict, and to wonder about, what will come next and prevents them from getting bored with hearing the same story repeatedly. The choice between building or bookending with a sensory story will depend on the people you are sharing the story with: will they need the repetition that comes from hearing the whole story every session? Will they be drawn in by wondering what happens next in a story that builds over time?

Calming

Sharing a sensory story can have a calming influence on learners (as long as you choose one that does not have sudden bangs in it). Having a relevant sensory story on hand as you teach a session can give you the opportunity to interrupt an activity that has become too raucous with a period of relevant reflection on the topic. Sensory stories can also be used in this way to facilitate transition between different sections of a session; getting everyone to stop and focus on a sensory story can help to change the mood of the room activity to focused independent work. Sensory work has been shown to have a positive effect on mood and behaviour so it is nice to use it as a route between activities or as a way to calm down and relax (Anderson *et al.* 2010; Ayer 1998; Fava and Strauss 2009; Hussein 2010; McCormack 2003; Murray *et al.* 2009).

Preparing

If you are planning a trip or a novel activity then using a sensory story to prepare individuals for what they will encounter will help them to process the new information that they gather as they complete that activity. Recently I had the pleasure of creating a sensory tour of the King's State Apartments at Kensington Palace. The Palace tour is a great example of a sensory story that can be used to prepare people for an experience. The experience of entering the Palace – the grandeur of the building, the richness of the colours of the walls and the paintings and the sound quality produced by the high ceilings and bare floors – is a very different experience from entering most rooms we frequent on a daily basis. Changes to what we are used to, produce anxiety and this can be heightened for individuals with special educational needs and disabilities. Anxiety inhibits our ability to learn. Knowing what to expect when we reach a location minimises our anxiety.

The sensory tour of Kensington Palace has ten parts, each of which relates to a location within the King's State Apartments. Each location has a short sentence or phrase that explains an aspect of history and an associated sensory experience. The sensory tour can be delivered away from the Palace, and when they experience it, learners are led through the experiences they can expect when they reach the Palace. Sharing this before their visit gives learners the opportunity to build up an understanding of what they will encounter, so when they arrive their anxiety about the unfamiliar place will be reduced. The tour they will take around the Palace will have the same phrases and experiences as the one they experienced in preparation, but delivered in situ the experiences will be bigger and richer allowing learners to experience awe in response to the remarkable rooms of the King's State Apartments.

Reinforcing memories

Individuals with learning disabilities may find laying down new memories difficult, for example, there is evidence that Down syndrome is associated with poor verbal short-term memory (Jarrold, Nadel and Vicari 2008) and that individuals with autism may experience difficulties with recalling personal memories (Boucher and Bowler 2011). Lee Swanson (1993) suggests that individuals with learning disabilities suffer from generalised working memory deficits, and Lacey (2009) speculates on how memory is affected in individuals with PMLD. Someone with a learning disability may be able to fully engage in, and enjoy, new experiences, but may not remember them a few days later.

Creating a sensory story out of an event gives you a tool that you can use to reinforce memories of what happened. Imagine a trip to a swimming pool: during the trip you will experience handing over money and being given a rubber wrist band, changing into your swimming costume whilst standing on ridged plastic mats, swimming – with the smell of chlorine and the sound of others splashing, having a hot shower and putting your wet swimming costume into a plastic bag. As each of these things occur you can take a moment to make everyone on the trip aware of them and make sure everyone has the experience – for example, by allowing each person to pay for their swim individually rather than paying for the group as a whole. You should clearly label each activity as it happens, for example, 'We are paying for our swim and being given a wrist band.' You should collect resources that will allow you to facilitate the experiences again when back at your base, such as asking the swimming pool if you can keep a wrist band or taking a sample of pool water home with you.

When you are back at your base you will be able to repeat the experiences and retell the event using the resources you collected. For example, 'We went to the swimming pool and paid to swim' – experience handing over money, 'We were given a wrist band' – experience putting on a wrist band, and so on. By repeating the account and the experiences you will help your experiencers to remember the activity.

Tasks to challenge higher ability learners

Creative writing challenges

You can use sensory stories as a stimulus for creative writing. Share a sensory story with your students so that they are familiar with what constitutes a sensory story.

ASK YOUR STUDENTS TO MAKE A SENSORY PLAN
FOR THEIR CREATIVE WRITING

Have your students think of a story they plan to write. This can be a story of their own creating or a story based on a familiar narrative. Ask them to write the title of the story in the centre of a page, and on radial lines around it write down each of the senses. They must then think of the sensory experiences that might be had within that story and write all their ideas down next to their associated sense. Once they have completed this plan they can write their story. This should lead to a beautiful piece of descriptive writing enriched with sensory detail.

CREATE A STORY BASED ON A SENSORY SEQUENCE

Present your students with a sequence of sensory experiences. Before sharing the experiences, tell them that they are going to write a story based upon what they experience. Your students must take in each experience and use their imaginations to think of what could be happening in the story to create that experience. Leave the stimuli laid out in sequential order for your students to re-experience as needed during their writing. This should result in some extraordinary pieces of imaginative writing.

CREATE A STORY BASED ON SENSORY PROMPTS

Give students a selection of sensory stimuli, and ask them to spend some time experiencing them and thinking about how they could be used within a story. Your students must then create a story based upon the experiences – they can use the experiences in any order and do not have to make use of all the experiences offered.

Distillation

Condensing a story down into ten sentences or fewer requires a high level of comprehension skills. To do this, a person must be able to identify: the key plot points in a story; the main characters; the central message or moral of the story; the genre of the story. Students must make tough judgements about what is essential to the narrative and what is not. Deciding what to leave out of a story is a high-level comprehension skill.

When you tell your students you want them to write a story in 'just' ten sentences they will think you are giving them an easy task and be happy to tackle it. Allow them plenty of time for the discussions they will need to have in order to decide what those ten sentences will be.

The ability to distil a large amount of information into a few phrases is a great revision skill. Once your students have their ten sentences you can ask them to think of sensory experiences for each sentence. Linking the sentences to sensory experiences will make them more memorable, so it is likely that your students will be able to memorise their ten-sentence version of the story. If a lot of thought has gone into deciding what those ten sentences are, in remembering the ten sentences they will probably be able to expand them to cover the important parts of the original story.

This activity does not need to be restricted to English literature; you can ask your students to summarise the content of their latest science module into ten sentences or to distil a historical story into ten sentences.

PART IV

Assessment

9

WHY ASSESS?

You do not fatten a pig by weighing it: progress is made whether or not it is measured. However, this does not mean that assessment is without its uses – a little assessment can be very helpful. In this chapter I am going to look at a number of uses for assessment and talk through some of the reasons you might have for assessing an individual's responses to sensory stories. Chapter 10 contains options for ways to assess the responses of the person with whom you are sharing sensory stories.

It is a part of your role

There are many roles where assessment is a requirement, for example, teachers are obliged by law to assess the progress of their students. Using assessment tools that are not flexible to the needs of individuals can be disheartening: you may know a student is making progress in small steps but only have a tool that measures large steps. The suggestions in Chapter 10 offer tools that can provide the necessary information and respond to the individual characteristics of individual learners.

It can help you reflect on what you are doing

Using an assessment tool can help you to reflect on what is taking place when you share a sensory story. An assessment tool can help you to be realistic if you have a tendency to be over-optimistic in your interpretations of an individual's responses and progress. Conversely, an assessment tool can open your eyes to an individual's progress if it is being made in very small steps that could go unnoticed.

Vlaskamp and Cuppen-Fonteine's study (2007) (mentioned on page 82), where staff were found to have little understanding of their clients' sensory needs and preferences, highlights how important it is for us to know the individual needs and abilities of the person with whom we are sharing sensory stories and also shows how simple assessments can illuminate things previously missed.

The assessment method suggestion on pages 83 and 84 is based on Vlaskamp and Cuppen-Fonteine's study and can be used to generate increased awareness and knowledge of an individual's needs and abilities.

An assessment that flags up a lack of progress can prompt us to consider whether there is some way we can change what we are doing so that the results of our input are improved. Profiling an individual using the assessment method on page 76 can help to furnish us with ideas about how to improve what we are doing.

Celebrate individuals' achievements

When a child is born, a path is laid out comprising steps they are expected to take – from sitting up unaided to walking, through to sitting their exams and leaving home. Along the way there are natural points of celebration – the first day of school, exam results, significant birthdays and so on. These causes for celebration serve a purpose beyond the recognition of each particular event; they are a chance for friends and family to gather and reinforce their bonds. It is an opportunity for that individual to receive and recognise the support from the community around them and to know that they are valued and appreciated by those people. This affects an individual's sense of identity as well as their self-esteem. The bonding, recognition and reinforcement of identity facilitated by celebrating an achievement are far more valuable than the swimming certificate or gold star, etc. that prompts them.

Parents of children with special educational needs and disabilities learn (as beautifully expressed in the poem 'Welcome to Holland' (Kingsley 1987)) that the path set out for their child is somewhat different to the standard one. Where that path is not clear they will have to navigate their own way and choose their own next steps.

Assessing using a measure that allows you to record significant steps in achievement creates the opportunity to celebrate progress as it is made.

The assessment method on page 76 provides levels of achievement that can be celebrated. You can download a certificate to award to individuals as they reach these levels from www.jkp.com/catalogue/book/9781849054843/resources.

Justify the use of sensory stories

An individual with a professional role may need to justify the expense of particular resources or the the expenditure of time or personnel on a particular activity. Assessment demonstrating that an activity has made an impact can provide the evidence needed to justify its ongoing use. That is a simple, pragmatic reason for the need for justification, but can also be useful to provide reassurance to parents and carers that they are doing the right thing.

10

ASSESSMENT METHOD SUGGESTIONS

As each person's path to learning is different, there can be no one right way of assessing progress, which is why I have presented the following as a set of suggestions. I hope that you will find something relevant to your needs or something that you can adapt to suit your particular circumstances. Do what is right for you and the person you care for.

P level questions

The following graded questions are based upon the P level descriptors. The P level descriptors are used in the UK for assessing students who have special educational needs and are achieving below what was National Curriculum Level 1. (The National Curriculum levels were abandoned in 2013 by the Coalition Government.)

You can use these questions as a summary assessment of where the person you are sharing stories with lies on the P levels. By ticking the questions to which you can answer 'yes', you will be able to see whereabouts on the scale of the P levels your story experiencer is. It is likely that you will have some ticks above their current level and that you will not tick some questions that are below their current level, but you can use the level that has the majority of the ticks as a guide. For example, if there were eight questions for each P level, and someone had ticked off four at P5, six at P6 and two at P7, they'd be considered to be operating at P6.

You can come back to these questions at regular intervals to assess whether there has been a change in your story experiencer's achievement. You can ask someone else to watch the story experiencer as you share the story with them and to tick off responses to certain questions. You may want to add detail to this assessment by asking them to make a note of the section of the story that prompted the response. It may also be interesting to see if the same questions are ticked off for different stories. If a person scores consistently over different stories then you can be reassured that you are estimating their level correctly. If they score highly for one story and not for another then you can question what it is about the two stories that causes the difference. If you record outcomes over time you may also be able to discover whether time of day/food/temperature, etc. has an influence on how a person responds to stories, for example, are they more likely to respond after dinner? Are they more responsive with a window open or with the heating on?

P level questions

P LEVEL 1

- Has the story experiencer encountered different experiences, for example, sight experiences or sound experiences?

- Does the story experiencer show a reflex response towards some stimuli, for example, flinching at a loud bang, jumping at a sudden sound or grimacing at a sour taste?

- Does the story experiencer occasionally seem aware of the story or the stimuli?

- Does the story experiencer seem to focus momentarily on aspects of the story or on particular stimuli?

- Does the story experiencer sometimes react during the storytelling? (Any reaction counts, so it could be that they vocalise, wave their arms, move their bodies, turn their heads or close their eyes – you will not necessarily know whether their reactions are in response to the story or to something else.)

P LEVEL 2

- Has the story experiencer begun to develop a pattern to their responses to experiencing the story, for example, always making a noise in response to certain part of the story or always turning their head away during a particular experience? These responses do not need to be consistent over all tellings of the story, they just need to be an emerging pattern, for example, often (but not always) turning their head in response to light stimuli.

- Is the story experiencer reacting to the story in some way? You are looking for reactions that are more than reflexes, for example, starting at a sudden noise would be a reflex, but moving in response to music is a reaction.

- Does the story experiencer show interest in parts of the storytelling process, for example, looking at the storyteller or reaching for an object?

- Will the story experiencer allow the story sharer to help them engage with the sensory stimuli, for example, by allowing a taste to be placed against their lips or by allowing their hand to be lifted onto a touch experience?

- Is the story experiencer sometimes proactive in their response to the story, for example, reaching for a favourite stimuli or making sounds from a favourite part of the story?

- Are the story experiencer's preferences being consistently expressed, for example, do they always smile in response to a particular stimuli or withdraw their hand from another?

- Does the story experiencer appear to recognise parts of the story or the storytelling process, for example, recognising the box the story is kept in, recognising the person telling the story or recognising particular stimuli within the story?

- Does the story experiencer persist in attempts to interact with stimuli, for example, trying to press a switch to turn on a light but missing and so trying again?

- Does the story experiencer remember particular responses for a little while, for example, remembering the refrain from 'Seasoned with Spice' or looking happy when they know they are going to be offered a sweet taste?

- Does the story experiencer help the story sharer to support them to interact with a stimulus, for example, if the story sharer is lifting the story experiencer's hand so that they can touch a stimulus, does the story experiencer also try and lift their hand a little?

P LEVEL 3

- Does the story experiencer sometimes show signs of trying to communicate intentionally, for example, vocalising towards a particular person or making gestures to direct attention?

- Is the story experiencer able to communicate consistent preferences as they experience the sensory story, for example, do you know that they dislike a particular smell or favour a particular sound? It does not matter how they communicate this information to you.

- Is the story experiencer able to make requests in their own way, for example, making an excited noise in response to a particular stimulus or looking eagerly in a particular direction?

- Is the story experiencer active in shared exploration of stimuli, for example, as they are being supported to touch or taste something do they make movements aimed at accomplishing the task at hand?

- Does the story experiencer concentrate for brief periods of time?

- Is the story experiencer interested in their engagement with sensory stimuli, for example, after feeling a sticky touch experience do they look at their hand to see what is on it or do they explore a touch experience with their fingers or by bringing it to their mouth to touch it with their lips?

- Does the story experiencer show signs of remembering aspects of the story, for example, do they put their hands ready to receive a touch experience in response to the auditory cue (the sentence) that precedes that experience or do they vocalise with a particular rhythm or tone during a particular section of the story on several retellings?

- Does the story experiencer use a few elements of conventional communication, for example, nodding or shaking their head, waving or making sounds for 'hello'?

- Does the story experiencer greet people they know in their own way?

- Does the story experiencer attempt to initiate activities or interactions, for example, making noises or responses from the story in an attempt to have the story told or reaching for someone's hand in an attempt to get them to join in with a touch experience?

- Can the story experiencer remember parts of the story, or responses to the story, over several tellings, for example, beginning to smile in anticipation of a favourite part of the story or vocalising parts of the story (the story experiencer does not need to be saying the actual worlds, just making their own vocalisations that relate to that part of the story)?

- Does the story experiencer anticipate events within the story, for example, in a story with a loud noise in it do they put their fingers over their ears before the sound occurs? Their actions do not need to be as structured as this; it may be that they flinch in response to the sound when they hear it the first time but during later tellings flinch in anticipation of the sound before it has been made?

- Can the story experiencer respond to options or choices, for example, choosing which story to read through gesture, gaze or vocalising?

- Does the story experiencer actively explore stimuli, for example, rolling a taste around their mouth, turning their head to hear sound in different ways, exploring a touch experience with their fingers, skin or lips, gazing intently at a sight experience or following a smell with their nose?

- Does the story experiencer attempt to solve problems they encounter using the resources at hand to them, for example, when attempting to use a switch to cause a light to come on do they push it towards an adult in the hope that they will operate the switch?

Beyond P level 3, jumps in achievement begin to be easier to identify. I am going to provide brief questions here to help you identify a level for your story experiencer; you may be able to add other achievements into this ladder of progression.

P LEVEL 4

- Is the story experiencer able to use single words, signs or symbols?

- Does the story experiencer understand simple communications, for example, 'clap' or 'look'?

- Does the story experiencer listen and respond to familiar stories?

P LEVEL 5

- Can the story experiencer combine two words together to communicate meaning, for example, 'more sweets'?

- If they are not understood does the story experiencer attempt to make themselves understood by repeating what they have said/signed/communicated with symbols?

- Can the story experiencer answer questions about things that are happening now, for example, 'Where is the light?'?

- Can the story experiencer follow simple instructions, for example 'Put it in the box'?

- Can the story experiencer derive some meaning from familiar symbols or pictures?

- Can the story experiencer make choices between things that represent other things, for example, picking a story by choosing between the boxes the stories are kept in?

P LEVEL 6

- Does the story experiencer start simple conversations?

- Does the story experiencer ask simple questions about the story?

- Can the story experiencer respond to others who are sharing the story, for example, receiving a stimulus that is being passed around a small group?

- Can the story experiencer follow instructions that have three key parts in them, for example, 'Put the ball in the blue box' (where there is a choice of objects and more than one coloured box)?

- Can the story experiencer recognise a few words or symbols that refer to familiar things to them?

P LEVEL 7

- Can the story experiencer construct basic phrases to communicate about things they are interested in?

- Can the story experiencer converse in a simple way about the story with another person or with a few other people?

- Does the story experiencer attend to the story for a short while?

- Can the story experiencer follow instructions with four key parts?

- Can the story experiencer respond to questions about the story?

- Can the story experiencer fill in a missing word if the story sharer pauses?

- Does the story experiencer appear interested in reading?

P LEVEL 8

- Has the story experiencer got a range of vocabulary they can choose from when they want to communicate?

- Can the story experiencer pretend to be a character in a story and join in with role-play?

- Can the story experiencer respond to questions that begin with 'why' or 'how'?

- Does the story experiencer understand that words, symbols and pictures convey meaning?

- Is the story experiencer able to recognise a number of familiar words or symbols?

The above questions are all based on the P levels for English. For some stories you may find it interesting to consider whether your story experiencer is achieving in other subject areas, for example science or food technology.[4]

Getting to know you questions

These questions can be used to build up a picture of your story experiencer's sensory preferences and abilities. Using these questions prior to telling a story can help you to think about how you can best facilitate the stimuli with your story experiencer. These questions may also help to highlight gaps in your knowledge about your story experiencer – if you re-ask yourself these questions after sharing sensory stories with your story experiencer for a little while then you may notice your own knowledge has increased. These questions are based upon Vlaskamp and Cuppen-Fonteine's study (2007). Vlaskamp and Cuppen-Fonteine discovered that simple questionnaires can help people who work with individuals with PMLD identify gaps in their knowledge about the people with whom they work. The researchers noted that once these gaps in knowledge were identified, people tended to go about filling them without any additional training being given; simply asking questions proved to be an effective way of improving provision for individuals with PMLD.

Do not worry if you cannot answer every question. Simply answer as best you can, and then come back to the questions after a period of sensory storytelling and see if you are now able to answer more comprehensively.

---

4   You can access the full P levels at www.government/publications/p-scales-attainment-targets-for-pupils-with-sen.

Getting to know you questions

1. What is your story experiencer's vision like?
   For example, what is the range of their vision? Does the position of objects affect their ability to see them? Does the amount of light or contrast with the background affect their ability to see?

2. What is your story experiencer's hearing like?
   For example, do they respond differently to different pitches? Do they prefer a certain volume? Are they responsive to longer or shorter bursts of sound?

3. What is your story experiencer's tactile sense like?
   For example, do they avoid touching particular items? Do they have particular touch preferences?

4. What is your story experiencer's taste like?
   For example, do they recognise particular flavours? Do they avoid particular tastes? Do they have strong reactions to particular flavours?

5. What are your story experiencer's motor skills like?
   For example, can they grab an object? Can they hold onto an object once they have it? Are they able to manipulate an object?

6. Does your story experiencer have particular sensory preferences?
   For example, are they more responsive to sound, taste, touch, sight or smell?

7. Are your story experiencer's reactions altered by their location?
   For example, do they respond more in a particular location? Are there places where they seem particularly withdrawn or passive?

8. How long does your story experiencer need to be able to react to a stimulus and, further to this, how long do they need to be able to respond to a stimulus?
   For example, how long does it take your story experiencer to move their body in response to a stimulus? How long after holding an item before your story experiencer begins to explore it?

9. Is your story experiencer affected by their body position?
   For example, are they more responsive when standing, sitting or lying down? Are they more responsive when sat beside you or sat opposite you?

10. Is your story experiencer more reactive at particular times of day?
    For example, is your story experiencer more alert in the morning? Is your story experiencer less alert after eating?

11. Is your story experiencer more alert after particular therapies?
    For example, are they more engaged after time in a sensory room, or tired after physiotherapy.

Reactions

Noticing over several tellings of the story when an individual reacts or responds can build a picture of progress. For example, if the first time you tell the story your story experiencer waves their arm at one point and does not respond during the rest of the story, you may wonder if their arm wave was anything to do with the story at all. If on subsequent retellings you notice that the arm wave always happens at the same point in the story, you can be more sure that it is in response to the story, or if their arm waving increases over subsequent tellings, this could be a sign that their involvement with the story is increasing.

Recording responses as they happen is tricky, as you will already have your hands full with the stimuli, so a simple chart where all you have to do is make a mark can be helpful.

The T bar chart can be used to do this (see Figure 10.1). The long horizontal bar is divided into sections representing of each section of the story. The vertical bar can be used for intentional/unintentional or positive/negative responses. If using it for intentional/unintentional responses, when your story experiencer responds to an item in the story in an intentional way, for example, grabbing a particular object and trying to use it, you would make a mark high up on the chart, level with the section of the story where that response occurred. If your story experiencer makes a move that you think is intentional, but you are less sure, you would place the mark relating to that response closer to the midline of the chart.

The same applies for positive/negative responses. These can be thought of as likes and dislikes, so if you get a big negative response to a stimulus, for example, spitting out the taste of lemons, the mark would be made very low on the chart, parallel to the section of the story indicated on the horizontal bar.

If you want to be ambitious you could record the story section, positive/negative response *and* whether it is intentional/unintentional, for example, by making a cross mark for intentional and drawing a dot for unintentional whilst using the vertical scale to indicate positive/negative. In a similar manner you could devise a code for yourself that indicates what sort of response you received, for example writing a 'V' on the chart to mark a vocalisation or a little eye symbol to mark eye contact with a stimulus.

It is a simple chart but you can use it swiftly to capture a lot of information and using it on repeated tellings might reveal information to you that you would not necessarily spot – for example, you may notice that movements that seemed random actually occur at the same part of the story on each telling and are a consistent response not a random action.

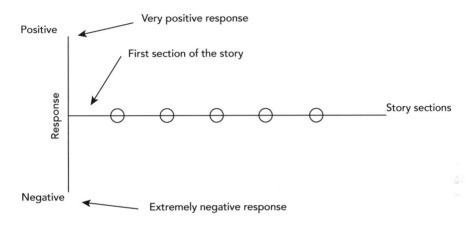

Figure 10.1 Reactions Chart

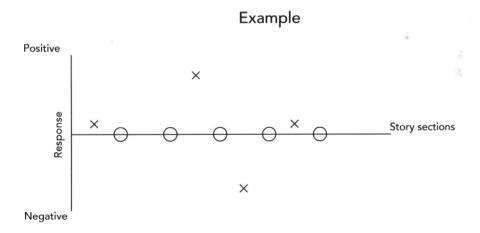

Figure 10.2 Completed Reactions Chart

This story experiencer responded to the story beginning, really enjoyed the third section, but was distressed by the fourth. They also showed a response during the fifth section of the story.

Target behaviour

If you know your story experiencer quite well then you may be on the lookout for certain target behaviours during a story sharing experience. Target behaviours could be things like vocalisations, expressions of clear preferences, exploring objects with greater concentration, tracking a moving object with their eyes, accepting participation without turning away or focusing on stimuli, for example, concentrating on a sound or staring at an object. This is by no means a comprehensive list; the behaviour that you look out for will be personal to the individual you are sharing the story with and best chosen as a target by, or in discussion with, someone who knows them well. The P level questions could also provide ideas for possible target behaviours to spot.

Once you have identified a target behaviour you can use an L shaped chart similar to those in Figures 10.3 on page 8 to track its occurrence throughout a storysharing session. By printing multiple L charts onto a single piece of A4 and recording your story experiencer's responses over time you will create a picture of how their responses have changed over successive story sharing sessions, which can be read at a glance.

A chart like this is very simple to use; you need only make a mark on it during the story as you see the target behaviour, but it can yield a lot of insight, for example, you may pick the target behaviour to make eye contact with an object and find that initially this only happens for objects that are meant as visual stimuli, but that after several tellings of the story your story experiencer is also focusing their eyes on other stimuli, such as watching a bell as you ring it. You may then start to think about considering whether your story experiencer is able to track objects as they move. Making little notes underneath your L charts can help you to remember insights like this and will inform what behaviours you choose as targets in the future.

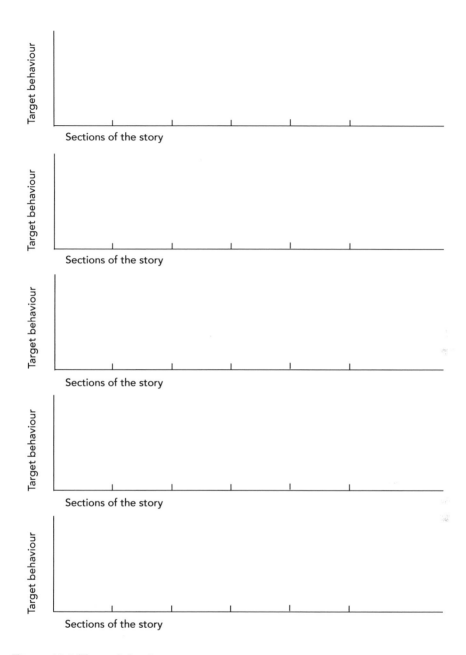

Figure 10.3 Target behaviour

Multiple targets

Using the L shaped chart (Figure 10.3) to track target behaviour is very simple and it may be that after a little while of using it you feel you would be able to do a little more. If this happens you might consider tracking multiple targets over a storytelling session. A nice thing to do can be to pick three progressive targets: one you think your story experiencer is very likely to display, one you think they might display if things go well and an ambitious one that you hope they will display but it would be a big event if they did, for example, making sound, making a sound with a similar rhythm to the sound in the story and making a sound that is recognisable as a word; or moving, moving with some intention in a particular direction and moving to do a particular task, such as picking up, kicking or pushing an item.

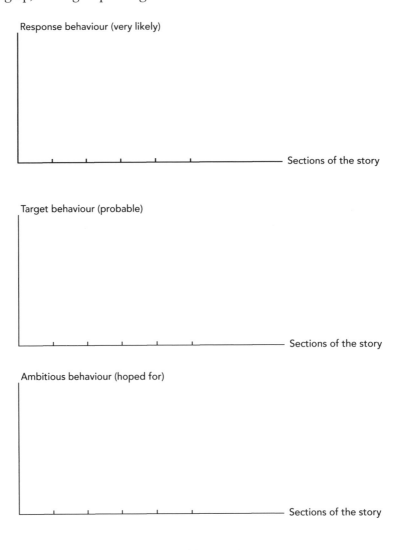

Figure 10.4 Target behaviour

Making these recordings over several tellings of a story can help to build up a picture changing responses over time.

It can also be interesting to do recordings of reactions at different times during the day, you may find that your story experiencer is more of a morning person or is more receptive in the evenings. Think about what might be influencing their responses – if you notice they are more responsive in the evening, you might consider whether this is because of the time of day, because of what went before or because of the low lighting? If you can identify these influences then you will be able to share stories with your story experiencer at the time when they are most able to engage with them.

Responses to different stories

Recording how your story experiencer responds to different stories can give you information about their preferences and about how they are responding to stories.

Keep a record of the stories you have shared and the responses received during their sharing. You may notice a steady increase or a general trend towards increasing responsiveness over the stories. This could indicate that your story experiencer is getting used to sensory stories and enjoying engaging with them. If you get high responses in one story but not in another, thinking about the differences between these stories will be interesting and could inform future choices you make on behalf of the story experiencer. You may notice that you get a high response to stories that are sung; this could lead you to choose more musical stories in future, but it could also lead you to creating little ditties about daily life to help facilitate everyday activities.

Recording responses in a simple graph can give you an at-a-glance comparison between stories.

The crossover between the target behaviour and the story creates a box of space on this graph. To record responses you could either enter a number in this space, for example, if your story experiencer displayed target behaviour one ten times during the telling of 'Seasoned with Spice', you could enter a '10' in this box; alternatively you could make a corresponding number of marks, for example, entering ten little crosses into the box – doing it this way may be more time consuming but will create a stronger visual representation of the information that will be easier to read at a glance. Another option would be to create a colour scale, for example, if the behaviour occurs fewer than five times the box would be coloured red, orange for between five and ten times and green for over ten times.

Figure 10.5 Responses to different stories

Responses to particular senses

Understanding whether your story experiencer is more responsive to particular senses can be useful information not only for informing your choice of future story, but also for choosing day-to-day activities, for example, if they are more responsive to sound stimuli then offering them choices through the day based on sounds might be more meaningful to them than offering them visual choices, such as pictures or symbols.

You can use a simple chart to record responses in relation to senses. You could create a new chart on each telling of a story or simply add to the existing chart to build a picture over time. It might be that on one telling of a story no one sense stands out as being particularly significant but that over time the small differences build up to a bigger, more noticeable one. You could record each telling in a different colour so that you can track individual tellings as well as an overall picture.

To record responses in relation to stimuli, you would keep the chart to hand and when a response is received make a cross in the relevant sense column on the chart. If you are feeling ambitious you could create a code and use this to represent different types of response, for example, a tick for a verbal response, a cross for a physical response and so on.

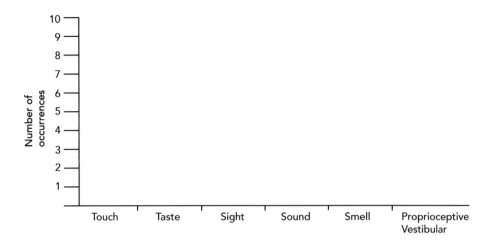

Figure 10.6 Responses to particular senses

PART V

The Sensory Stories and Associated Resources

11

ABOUT THE SENSORY STORIES
AND ASSOCIATED RESOURCES

This part of the book contains five sensory stories with ideas for activities that could be shared alongside the story. Within the stories and activities you will find songs and movement, as well as the rich sensory stimuli you expect. The activities were created with the classroom in mind, and so I refer to students, teachers, class, lessons, etc., but they could just as easily be used at home or in other group settings. The stories cover a purposefully broad spectrum of subjects from science fiction to traditional folklore. I hope you will be able to find a story to suit your story experiencer within them. More stories can be found at http://jo.element42.org.

The sensory stories and associated resources are presented in the following way:

The Story

- *Story text*: The text of the story is presented in a manner that should make it easy for you to photocopy and use. (The pages which can be photocopied are marked with a ★.)

- *About the story*: This contains an explanation of the story and aims to give you more background information to enable you to tell it in a meaningful way.

Resourcing the stimuli

- *Shopping list*: A basic list of what you will need for sharing the sensory story, ideal for copying down and creating a shopping list.

- *Detailed list*: A detailed account of each of the stimuli you will need, giving you extra information that will help inform your choices as you select stimuli for your story.

Facilitating the stimuli

- Guidance about how to facilitate the sensory stimuli.

Activities

- *Exploration*: These activities give ideas for exploration, often sensory, which can develop a person's connection with, or understanding of, the story.

- *Creative*: These activities are creative ways of engaging with the topics presented within the story.

- *Discovery*: These activities offer ways to build learning using the story as a starting point.

- *A series of six lessons based upon the story*: The lessons are based upon the bookending structure of using a sensory story. Research (PAMIS 2002; Young and Lambe 2011) has indicated that the benefits gained from repeating sensory stories peak around the eight repetition mark. The notion of eight repetitions being the ideal should be taken as a guide not a rule; each student will respond differently. Six lessons provide students with the chance to encounter the story twelve times; this should be enough to give time to respond to those who may need more than eight repetitions whilst the diversity of activities within the lessons should hold the attention of those who need fewer repetitions. Adapt the lessons to suit your particular students.

The lesson sequences provided focus on the following areas of learning.

- 'The Selkie Wife': PE, dance.

- 'Seasoned with Spice': Design and Technology, cooking.

- 'Two People Made Me': Science, life cycles.

- 'To the Centre of the Earth!': Science, materials.

- 'The Forest of Thorns': Literacy, traditional tales.

All of the stories can be used in multiple subject areas. For example, 'Two People Made Me' would fit into PSHE (personal social and health education) as well as science. 'To the Centre of the Earth!' could fit into geography, English or science. Many of the associated resources for each story contain songs and movement sequences, giving you options for engaging your students in the story through music or movement. The overlapping of the stories between subject areas creates plenty of opportunities for cross-curricular study.

★

THE SELKIE WIFE

*When the moon is bright and full
Selkies swim to shore
To shed their skins and dance.
A man once spied the Selkies dancing and
    wanted one to be his wife. He stole a
    discarded Selkie skin and locked it in a
    box.
At dawn their dancing was done, the Selkies
    dived back into the waves and were
    gone.
One Selkie could not find her skin, she wept
    as her friends left without her.
The man comforted the crying Selkie and
    asked her to be his wife.
The Selkie was happy being married to the
    man, but at night the smell of the ocean
    floated through her open window and
    she longed to be with her friends.
Many years later the Selkie found the box
    with her skin inside, without a second
    thought she slipped it on and swam
    away to dance on distant shores with
    her friends.*

About the story

This story is an old story. It has been told many times in many different ways. Tales of mysterious women are common to mariners. I grew up on a boat and remember my father pointing out seals to our crew, suggesting they might be beautiful women basking on the rocks. Selkies are found in Scottish folklore and by other names in other seafaring lands. In some versions of the story, the man does not know his wife is a Selkie. In others, the Selkie gives birth to a child and the decision to leave for the sea again is made all the harder. In some, the Selkie rescues the man from drowning. However, in all the stories, the Selkie faces the choice of having legs and walking on the land or having a tail and swimming in the sea.

Woven into the few sentences of the story are some lovely messages to share with story experiencers.

- The man watches the Selkies who move in a way that is different to the way he moves, and he sees that movement as beautiful. Many of us move in different ways - some might have limited movements, some jerky movements or twitches or some might be on wheels. The man saw difference as beautiful. We can all find beautiful ways to move.

- The Selkie, in this story unwillingly but in other stories willingly, gives up her true identity to be with the man. She is able to be happy living on land for a while, but in the end she has to go back to being a Selkie - to being her true self. We may be able to change to suit the needs and desires of others for a while - we may even be able to do so with a smile on our faces - but in the long run each one of us needs to find our own way to being ourselves and expressing ourselves in a way that makes us joyful, just as the Selkie expresses herself by dancing with her friends.

Resourcing the stimuli
Shopping list

- Silver tights/stockings

- LED lamp

- White tracing paper/tissue paper

- ▲ Music
- ▲ A box
- ▲ A pipette or a drinking straw

Optional

- ▲ A toy tambourine and some coloured ribbons
- ▲ Wet rags or pebbles
- ▲ Access to the internet or a CD of the Wedding March

Detailed list

Prior to beginning the story.

SIGHT AND TOUCH

A pair of silvery tights: the tights are going to represent the skin of a fish so look for something that will look slippery and silvery like a fish's tail. Cut the tights in half so that each leg is separate or buy stockings!

When the moon is bright and full

SIGHT

A round white light source: LED lamps are ideally suited to this, or a torch would work. You can choose to make your light source more moonlike by cutting out a disc of white tracing paper or tissue paper and attaching this to the front of the light source.

Selkies swim to shore

TOUCH

A washing-up bowl or a water tray filled with cool (but not too cold) water.

To shed their skins and dance.

TOUCH AND SOUND

Music: a Celtic jig would be appropriate music for Selkies to dance to; alternatively you can personalise this story to your particular Selkie story experiencer and choose music that will make them want to dance.

You can accentuate the music by providing a hoop with ribbons and bells attached to it for the story experiencer to wave as they dance. If you cannot find one of these you could tie a few coloured ribbons onto the edge of a toy tambourine.

A man once spied the Selkies dancing and wanted one to be his wife. He stole a discarded Selkie skin and locked it in a box.

TOUCH AND SIGHT

Find a sturdy box. This is the box that the man will keep the Selkie's skin hidden in for years, so if you are able to find a box with a lock, or paint the inside of the box so that it looks dark and mysterious, this will add to the experience of the story.

At dawn their dancing was done, the Selkies dived back into the waves and were gone.

SOUND

You can make the splashing noises you will need by simply slapping the water in the washing-up bowl with your palm; alternatively drop a succession of objects into the water – wet balls of fabric or pebbles would be ideal.

One Selkie could not find her skin, she wept as her friends left without her.

TOUCH

You can buy cheap small pipettes online; you might also find them in hardware stores or in pharmacies. If you cannot find a pipette, you can use a drinking straw instead. To use a drinking straw, submerge one end of the straw half a centimetre in water and place your finger over the other end of the straw. When you lift the straw out of the water you will have a drip of water trapped inside the end. To release this water droplet onto the face of the story experiencer, remove your finger from the end of the straw.

The man comforted the crying Selkie and asked her to be his wife.

TOUCH AND SOUND

Delivering the comforting touch experience needs no resource other than you. To represent the happy occasion of marriage you can play a peal of church bells – as this is difficult to buy, I recommend looking for something suitable online on YouTube or SoundCloud. An alternative would be to play the Wedding March, which you may be able to find in different formats in music shops.

> *The Selkie was happy being married to the man, but at night the smell of the ocean floated through an open window and she longed to be with her friends.*

SMELL AND TOUCH

Keep your chosen sea smell sealed in a plastic container; by doing this you will allow the air inside the container to become fragranced thus amplifying the experience of the smell. There are a number of ways you could create the smell of the sea: you can buy essential oils that are meant to represent the smell of the ocean – a few drops of one of these on a cotton pad would work; alternatively, a little bit of fish or seaweed would give off an appropriate odour.

> *Many years later the Selkie found the box with her skin inside, without a second thought she slipped it on and swam away to dance on distant shores with her friends.*

TOUCH, SIGHT AND SOUND

No new resources are needed for this final sentence.

Facilitating the stimuli

> *Prior to beginning the story.*

Help the story experiencer to pull the legs of the tights over their hands and arms. This can be done as you announce the name of the story. Seeing the silvery tights and being helped to put them on can act as a sensory cue for the story that is about to be shared.

> *When the moon is bright and full*

Hold the light representing the moon steadily within the gaze of the story experiencer. If you are looking to encourage tracking you can allow the moon to rise during the sentence: hold it with your arm outstretched and parallel to the floor and gradually raise it upwards, keeping your arm straight as you do so, to mimic the curved transit of the moon across the sky (to lift it straight up would make it look as if the moon arrived at it is zenith in a lift).

Selkies swim to shore

Support the story experiencer in plunging their arms (clad in tights) into the water. Once submerged, your story experiencer can make a doggy paddle or breast-stroke motion.

To shed their skins and dance.

Peel the wet tights off the story experiencer's arms as the music begins to play. You can give the story experiencer a hoop with ribbons and bells tied to it so that they can join in the dancing.

A man once spied the Selkies dancing and wanted one to be his wife. He stole a discarded Selkie skin and locked it in a box.

Support the story experiencer in picking up the wet tights and dropping them into the box. Close the lid on the box and, if it has a lock, lock it up.

At dawn their dancing was done, the Selkies dived back into the waves and were gone.

Create a series of splashing sounds to represent the Selkies diving into the water. You can do this by slapping the water with your hand or by dropping a series of objects into the water.

One Selkie could not find her skin, she wept as her friends left without her.

Use the pipette to drip tears onto the face of the story experiencer. Make sure you are using a clean pipette or straw and clean water. Aim for the skin of the cheek near the nose – along the path a tear would follow were it to fall from a crying eye.

The man comforted the crying Selkie and asked her to be his wife.

If it is appropriate for you to do so, you may hug the story experiencer in a comforting way. Other comforting gestures might be more appropriate, for example, laying a hand over the story experiencer's hand or clasping their shoulder. If you are able to provide a peal of wedding bells these can ring out as the sentence ends.

The Selkie was happy being married to the man, but at night the smell of the ocean floated through an open window and she longed to be with her friends.

Hold the smell to the side of the story experiencer just out of their vision, and use a small fan or sheet of paper to gently waft the scent towards them. Be sure to waft gently otherwise you may just blow the smell past the story experiencer without giving them the time to fully appreciate it.

Many years later the Selkie found the box with her skin inside, without a second thought she slipped it on and swam away to dance on distant shores with her friends.

There are many ways to facilitate the final sentence of this story in a sensory way; you might choose the one most appropriate to your story experiencer or opt to do several.

- You can grab the wet skin from inside the box.

- You can pull the wet fabric back onto your arms.

- You can 'swim' again in the washing-up bowl or water tray.

- You can play the music that played during the dancing earlier – very quietly at first, as though far away, and gradually getting louder.

Exploration activity
Sensory seaside

Create a sensory exploration tray that represents the seaside where the Selkies danced. Consider including shells and pebbles, sand, seaweed, water, etc. You can play dancing music as you explore the different experiences in the tray.

Separating the items into different bowls can allow you to explore the different sensory aspects of this story in a small space, for example, on a lap tray. If you cannot go to the seaside to collect a bowl of seaweed, try using salted spaghetti strands instead – if you cook the spaghetti in water with a few drops of green food colouring then you can create a seaweed-coloured touch experience.

You can freeze your seaside ingredients in a tub of water and then present them either as a block of ice, or smash the ice with a hammer and present them amongst the slush to be explored.

Creative activities

Movement

You can explore movement by finding different ways to move your body; you can also explore movement by being interested in how others move and finding out how it feels to move in that way by mimicking their movements. Here are some ideas for how to do this.

If I was... places

The Selkies in the story move differently depending on where they are – in the water they swim and on land they dance.

Find images of different places (or sounds from different places) and use these as prompts for your movement. Here are some examples:

- Desert sand: how would you move through deep, slippery desert sand?

- The calm sea: how would you move through a calm sea – would you move in such a way as to try not to disturb it?

- A rough sea: how would your body respond to being buffeted by the waves?

- Hot volcanic rock: how would you move across a hot surface?

- Space: how would you move in an environment with no gravity?

Once you are good at making up lots of different movements you can perform them in a sequence to create a modern dance piece. You could add music and sounds relevant to the places to your dance.

If I was... animals

Animals move in lots of different ways.

Use images of animals, or the sounds made by animals, as prompts for movement. Here are some examples:

    ⚲ A hummingbird: can you move so fast that your limbs are a blur?

    ⚲ A snake: can you move without using your arms or legs?

    ⚲ A panther: can you move in a slinky, sleek way?

    ⚲ A cormorant: can you bob about almost still and then suddenly dive and glide?

You can develop this activity by looking at the life cycle of a particular animal and creating movements to suit all the stages of its life. These movements can be performed in sequence to create a dance piece.

If I was… imagination

Invent rules for the ways your body can move. Here are some examples:

    ⚲ If my elbows were made of jelly I'd move like this…

    ⚲ If I had two arms growing out of my head, but none on my body, I'd move like this…

    ⚲ If my feet were made of ice, I'd move like this…

    ⚲ If the floor were very sticky, I'd move like this…

    ⚲ If my body did not bend, I'd move like this…

If I was… you

For this version of 'If I was' you need to be in a group of friends. If you have not got a group you can explore movement with, you might be able to use the internet to get ideas for people who move in different ways.

Take it in turns to copy the movement of your friends. You are not doing this to make fun of their movement but to find out what it feels like to move as they do.

If your friends have particular skills that they can perform – for example, martial arts, dance or swimming – perhaps they can teach you some of the movements from those things. If your friends have limitations on their movements, taking time to understand how this feels physically can help you to feel closer to them. Remember, everyone can move in a way that is beautiful – by exploring each other's movements you can discover new ways of being beautiful.

Sequencing movements

With all of the 'If I was' games there are opportunities to sequence the movements. Sequencing and rehearsing a sequence of movements is not only good for the body, but can also help to improve the memory. You can create a sequence in the same way as you would play a memory game such as, 'I went to the shops and I bought…' Try an imaginary journey on which you see a lot of animals, for example:

Person 1: 'I went on an adventure and I saw a hummingbird,' – flap arms very fast.

Person 2: 'I went on an adventure and I saw a snake,' – slither on the floor, 'and a hummingbird,' – flap arms very fast.

Person 3: 'I went on an adventure and I saw a dolphin,' – jump and then undulate your body as if swimming butterfly stroke, 'and a snake,' – slither on the floor, 'and a hummingbird,' – flap arms very fast, etc.

Performing the movements will make it easier to remember the animals encountered on the adventure.

You can create a sequence of movements to tell the Selkie story. Invent your own or use the suggestions below.

When the moon is bright and full

Begin curled up in a tight ball on the floor, uncurl and stretch your arms wide and open to be the bright fullness of the moon.

Selkies swim to shore

Move around the space as if swimming.

To shed their skins and dance.

Imagine you are peeling yourself out of your skin – begin at your ribs and roll your imagined skin all the way down to your toes, step out of it and dance.

A man once spied the Selkies dancing and wanted one to be his wife. He stole a discarded Selkie skin and locked it in a box.

Creep about as if sneaking through the dance to steal the skin.

At dawn their dancing was done, the Selkies dived back into the waves and were gone.

Dance, look up suddenly as if spotting the rising sun, leap as if diving into water, and then move in swimming movements again.

One Selkie could not find her skin, she wept as her friends left without her.

Imagine you are the one Selkie left behind on the beach – run frantically from side to side, stop and swing your arms around as if asking anyone where your skin could be, before falling to your knees and hiding your eyes as if crying.

The man comforted the crying Selkie and asked her to be his wife.

If you are doing these movements with a friend one of you can play the part of the man and comfort the Selkie on her knees. If you are performing alone you can join this section of the story to the next section.

The Selkie was happy being married to the man, but at night the smell of the ocean floated through her open window and she longed to be with her friends.

Move as if doing household chores and look happy. Lie down as if to sleep but toss and turn restlessly, and then get up to lean out of a window. Imagine yourself carried away in your movements by moving around the space, rising and falling as if carried away by waves.

Many years later the Selkie found the box with her skin inside, without a second thought she slipped it on and swam away to dance on distant shores with her friends.

Mime opening a box and look surprised. Roll your skin on from your toes to your ribs and then leap and swim and dance jubilantly.

If you are performing this movement sequence with friends then you can each take different roles and turn the dance into a play.

Discovery activities
Losing, hiding and finding
One of the themes of this story is loss. We have all had experiences of losing things, some of them big, some of them small.

Finding

Playing games that involve searching for lost things can be a lot of fun. In the sensory story the Selkie's lost skin is represented by a pair of silvery tights. You could play hide and seek with the tights. One person pretends to be the man and the other the Selkie. Whilst the Selkie is not looking the man hides her skin (the tights) somewhere in the room. It is then the Selkie's job to find the tights.

Hiding

Object permanence – knowing that an object is still there when we cannot see it anymore – is part of the development of our understanding. Hiding an object in a box that your story experiencer can see and then allowing them to open the box and find the object reinforces object permanence. Exploring boxes to find out what is inside can be a fun extension of this – use shredded paper or packing material to fill the box and then hide different things inside. You can choose things that provide a variety of sensory stimulation – try a lemon or orange with the rind removed for an interesting-to-touch, smelly object, sunglasses for a discoverable sight experience or a rattle or bell for a sound experience.

For more able story experiencers create personalised boxes in which to hide treasured possessions. Once you have got a box with treasure in, it is only natural to draw a treasure map to remind you of its hiding place. You can make a game for two players based on the battleships game, out of hidden treasure and maps. Here are how to do it.

Hidden treasure
PREPARATION

- Each player draws a grid eight squares wide and eight squares high.

- Label the squares along one axis with letters and the squares along the other axis with numbers. At this point both players' maps look the same.

- Each player has four boxes of treasure that they can hide anywhere on their map.

- Players must hide their maps from each other and not peak at each other's maps.

- ⤒ One treasure box is very big; it is three squares wide and three squares high. One treasure box is very small, it is just one square. The remaining boxes are medium sized; each one is two squares by two squares.

- ⤒ Players can, just for fun, draw other details on their grids to make them look more map-like.

PLAYING THE GAME

- ⤒ Once each player has hidden their treasure on their map the hunting can begin. Take it in turns to hunt for treasure by calling out a grid reference, for example, B3.

- ⤒ When one player calls out a grid reference the other player must look in that square and reply 'Treasure' if there is treasure in that square or 'Keep hunting' if there is not.

- ⤒ The player who called out the grid reference can make a mark on their map to remember which squares they have asked about – writing T in squares where treasure has been found and X in squares where there was no treasure can help them to keep track of their search.

- ⤒ The player who uncovers all of the other player's treasure first is the winner.

You can change the game by making your starting grid bigger or smaller and having more or less treasure. A big grid with a little treasure in will be very hard; a small grid with a lot of treasure will be very easy.

You can extend this game by requiring answering players to say how many squares away from treasure a certain square is. For example, if player one calls B3 and player two has no treasure in B3, but does have treasure buried four squares away they would respond 'four'.

Six lesson plans for 'The Selkie Wife'

This series of six lessons will engage your students in exploring movement and expressing themselves and narrative through movement. They will enable you to revisit 'The Selkie Wife' sensory story on multiple occasions building on previous learning with each revisit.

These lessons are intended to be PE/dance lessons so I recommend using a suitable space to deliver them in, for example, a school hall, sports hall or large empty space. You will need a few chairs and the sensory story resources to begin and end each session, but these can be stacked to the side to make space when you get to the main task section of each lesson.

The following lesson plans address PE/dance objectives but there is scope for using 'The Selkie Wife' story to address objectives in PSHE, Design and Technology, Music and Literacy. In PSHE you can talk about changing your behaviour to suit others. In Design and Technology you can create costumes for your dance. In music you can create music to dance to. In literacy you can look at traditional tales and folk stories from other cultures.

Lesson plan 1: Hiding and finding (1 hour)

This lesson will get students moving and thinking about different ways of expressing themselves using their bodies. It is based on the hiding and finding of the Selkie's skin in the story.

RESOURCES YOU WILL NEED FOR THIS LESSON

- ⅄ 'The Selkie Wife' sensory story and associated resources

- ⅄ Enough chairs for everyone to have a seat

- ⅄ Tambourine and a long ribbon – a ribbon on a stick such as is used in rhythmic gymnastics can be fun here

- ⅄ A box with a lid

- ⅄ A selection of items – try to include things that stimulate the senses: for example, smelly things, tasty things and sticky things!

- ⅄ A selection of hiding and sneaking music (e.g. the Pink Panther theme)

Optional

- ⅄ Boxes

PREPARATION

Set up the chairs in a circle, and place the resources for the sensory story somewhere where you will be able to reach them easily as you share the story.

OBJECTIVE

To express oneself using simple movements, and to respond to simple, movement-based instructions.

INTRODUCTION (15 MINUTES)

The cue for these six lessons can be used as a way of getting to the lesson location, so if you are moving from a classroom to a school hall this can be useful. If you are staying in the same room you can simply do a lap of the room and end up on the chairs. To deliver the cue you need a tambourine and a long ribbon. Play the tambourine and waft the ribbon behind you as you begin to move. Your class must catch onto the ribbon and follow you as you dance towards the chairs. Enjoy this cue – make it fun. You can spontaneously introduce an element of follow my leader as you do movements that inspire your class to copy you, for example, skipping, reaching high into the air, clapping or wiggling.

Once everyone has danced to their seats, allow a pause in readiness for the story. During this time your students can put the tights onto their arms as the story requires. The opening line of 'When the moon is bright and full' and its accompanying sight experience should complete the stilling of your students and create an atmosphere in which the story can be shared and appreciated.

GROUP TASK (10 MINUTES)

This activity is going to introduce the group to the idea that our physical responses convey information. You can demonstrate first and then invite students to have a go.

Hide something in the box. Place the box to one side and yourself to the other side.

Approach the box (you can change how you approach the box each time, for example, creeping, running or sauntering).

Open the box and react to what you see inside. Make your reactions big – use your whole body.

Return to your seat and show your students two objects. Can they identify which one was in the box based on the reaction they saw you give?

INDIVIDUAL/GROUP WORK (20 MINUTES)

Working individually, students should move about the space available, approaching boxes, opening them and reacting to their contents. Ideally the boxes will be imaginary, as will their contents, but some students may need concrete items to work with. If this is the case, you can scatter boxes around the room and place different items inside each box.

Opening the boxes works a bit like musical statues. You should play music for your students to move around to, encouraging them to move in a way that suits the music. Think about using music with different tempos to encourage your students to move at different speeds; think about music with changes in it to encourage changes in directions; think about music with high and low notes to encourage students to move high and low; music with sudden crashes and bangs could encourage jumping.

When the music stops, your students should imagine there is a box before them (or find a box if you are using real boxes). They should open the box and react to what is inside. Get them to 'freeze' their reactions and look around. Can you, or other students, guess what might be inside the boxes based on the reactions you see?

To develop this activity, split the class up and have each group watch the other. Ask students to identify things they liked about what they saw and incorporate them into their own movements.

PLENARY (15 MINUTES)

Choose one move that you saw and particularly liked from each student, or have students nominate moves. Get each student to perform their identified move and talk as a group about what is good about that move.

Share 'The Selkie Wife' sensory story together.

Lesson plan 2: Different movements (1 hour)

In this lesson students will think about how different environments and ways of being inspire different forms of movement. They will revisit concepts of movement, for example, stillness, shape, rhythm, speed, level, direction, etc. that they were introduced to in the first lesson.

RESOURCES YOU WILL NEED FOR THIS LESSON

- ⅄ 'The Selkie Wife' sensory story and associated resources

- ⅄ Chairs

ᐱ Images of different places and animals

ᐱ Tambourine and long ribbon to cue the lesson in with

PREPARATION

Arrange the chairs ready for sharing the sensory story. Place the images of different places and animals in the room where you will be exploring movement together.

OBJECTIVE

To use movement to respond to stimuli.

INTRODUCTION (15 MINUTES)

Cue the lesson using the same method as described in Lesson Plan 1, and share 'The Selkie Wife' sensory story together.

GROUP TASK (10 MINUTES)

Tell the students that they are going to recreate their day so far. How did their day start? It is likely everyone will have been asleep in bed, so ask everyone to lie on the floor as if they are sleeping. Students unable to lie on the floor can act as if they are fast asleep in their chairs.

Continue to explore the movements students have made through the day – perhaps stretching as they woke, rushing as they got ready for school, being jiggled up and down on the bus, carrying a bag, greeting friends, etc.

Explain to the students that how we move is dependent on who we are and where we are.

INDIVIDUAL/GROUP WORK (20 MINUTES)

Split the class into two groups. Give one group the images of places and the other the images of animals. Looking at each image in turn, the group members must invent movements they would make in that location or movements that animal would make.

After ten minutes stop the groups and ask one group to sit down. The standing group will then take it in turns to perform one of the movements they rehearse. The watching group must decide which image the performance relates to. A more fun, and more involved, way of doing this is to have the watching group stand in a line and when the performer from the performing group begins to move, the watching group form a line behind them and copy the movement. The watchers then get the visual experience of watching the movement and the physical experience of performing it themselves.

Switch the groups around and repeat.

PLENARY (15 MINUTES)

Reflect with the group on how many different movements they have created over this and the previous lesson. Ask if anyone can think of a move they have not made - any move at all! Take a few answers, and have students demonstrate their answers and then extend the question. Ask for a body shape that has not been made yet, a jump that has not been done yet, a way of travelling that has not been done yet, and so on. Focus also on the detail of movement - asking for a facial, hand or foot movement that has not been done yet. Students can join in at whatever level of movement is appropriate to them. Confirm that all sorts of movements are beautiful and interesting to watch.

Share 'The Selkie Wife' sensory story together.

Lesson plan 3: Mini sequences (1 hour)

In this lesson students will link movements together to create mini sequences, which they will try to remember, repeat and improve through the course of the lesson.

RESOURCES YOU WILL NEED FOR THIS LESSON

- ⌃ 'The Selkie Wife' sensory story and associated resources
- ⌃ Chairs
- ⌃ Tambourine and long ribbon
- ⌃ Images and stimuli used in previous lessons, plus any extra you want to include

Optional

- ⌃ Music to play in the background

PREPARATION

Set up the chairs and sensory story resources ready for sharing the sensory story.

Place the images and stimuli in the room where the movements will be performed.

OBJECTIVE

To link movements to form simple sequences.

INTRODUCTION (15 MINUTES)

Cue the lesson and share the sensory story as in previous lessons.

GROUP TASK (10 MINUTES)

In this lesson students are going to have to remember a sequence. Give everyone's memories a warm up by choosing three students to come to the front. Using the animal image cards give each student at the front an animal card. Say 'I saw a…' and then move along the line of students naming each animal. Have the students place their animal cards on the floor face down and create a little interlude – a snippet of music and a little boogie for everyone could be appropriate (try hand jive movements for those who are seated). Then ask the children who are seated if they can remember the animals of the students at the front. How do they do? If it is easy, create a longer string of animals.

Next ask students to come to the front. Present the cards as before, but this time ask each student to make a movement associated with their animal. Repeat the rest of the process. Did seeing a movement help students to remember the animals?

Repeat once more, but this time get the watching students to copy the animal movements made by the students at the front. Does this make it even easier to remember the sequence?

INDIVIDUAL/GROUP WORK (20 MINUTES)

Students can work on their own, in pairs or in small groups. They can use the image cards as stimuli or work from their own imaginations. Their task is to create a sequence of movements linked either to the cards or to stimuli from their imaginations and to remember this sequence. You can require a different number of movements from different students depending on their capability to remember (which you will have assessed during the previous activity).

Allow students time to plan, practise and rehearse their sequences and then stop everyone. Ask for a group or individual to volunteer to show their sequence. Let them introduce it by explaining what the movements will represent ahead of the performance, for example, 'I am going to move like a snake, then a tiger and then an elephant.' Get the rest of the class to give useful feedback on the performance, identifying what was good about it and giving suggestions as to how to make it better.

If there is time, groups could then pair up to watch and evaluate each other, or you can move around the room watching each group in turn and offering feedback.

PLENARY (15 MINUTES)

Can students remember their sequences? Have each group perform in turn and praise them on their ability to remember their sequence. The images can be used as prompts for people who forget. Talk about what movements were particularly good.

Share 'The Selkie Wife' sensory story together.

Lesson plan 4: Story sequence development (1 hour)

In this lesson students are going to use all the movement skills they have developed over the past few lessons, as well as their understanding of sequencing, to create a movement sequence based on 'The Selkie Wife' sensory story.

RESOURCES YOU WILL NEED FOR THIS LESSON

- ⌃ 'The Selkie Wife' sensory story and associated resources
- ⌃ Chairs
- ⌃ Box
- ⌃ Tambourine and long ribbon
- ⌃ Music to suit 'The Selkie Wife' story – this could be folk dancing music, soothing atmospheric wave music or wedding music

PREPARATION

Set up the chairs and the sensory resources ready for sharing the story.

OBJECTIVE

To use movement to imaginatively respond to stimuli and create simple sequences of different kinds of movement.

INTRODUCTION (15 MINUTES)

Cue the lesson and share the sensory story as usual.

GROUP TASK (10 MINUTES)

Revisit each of the sensory stimuli in the story by placing them in the box and having students approach the box and react to the contents as they did in Lesson Plan 1.

Explain that in this and the next lessons, the class are going to be creating movements to tell 'The Selkie Wife' story. Students have a choice between creating movements that enact what the people in the story would be doing or movements that are responses to the various stimuli. The first version will create a cross between a dance and a play; the latter version will create a piece of abstract dance based on the play. Students are free to do either, but it is probably best not to mix them up too much.

Revisit each section of the story text asking students to move in the way that the people in the story move at that time, for example, swimming, drifting around a house, dancing and walking down an aisle.

INDIVIDUAL/GROUP WORK (20 MINUTES)

Students can work on their own, in pairs or in small groups to come up with ideas; the whole class will be working at the same pace as you will be cuing in their movements.

Read each section of the story in turn and share the stimuli that accompanies it. Students respond by making up a movement to go with each section. If you find that the group naturally tends towards the play version of the sequence or the abstract version of the sequence then go with that; if there is a natural split then divide the class according to that split and allow two sequences to develop.

Take time as the movements are invented to invite feedback from peers and improve the movements.

For each section of the story choose one movement (or if working with two groups, two movements). It may well be that these movements are amalgamations of several movements, for example, 'Ooh shall we do X's leap, with Y's shape at the end?'

If creating movements is too much to be accomplished in the time allowed, then in this lesson you can introduce your students to the movements suggested on page 107 and in the following lesson you can work on evaluating and improving those movements.

PLENARY (15 MINUTES)

There has been a lot to cover in one session, so if you are not quite there yet do not worry. Remind students that this is going to be a project that lasts over three lessons, so it is okay if it is not yet clear. Go over what you have achieved so far – you might have a movement for each stage of the story or you might have only got part way through. Let your students know that in their next lesson they will be thinking about how to make these movements even better.

Share 'The Selkie Wife' sensory story together.

Note: It is important that you record the movements the students decided on for the story so that you are able to remind them in the next lesson if necessary.

Lesson plan 5: Evaluating and improving (1 hour)

In this lesson students are going to finalise their sequence of movements to tell the story of 'The Selkie Wife'; they will be supported in evaluating and improving their performance.

RESOURCES YOU WILL NEED FOR THIS LESSON

- ⅄ 'The Selkie Wife' sensory story and associated resources

- ⅄ Tambourine and ribbon

- ⅄ Chairs

- ⅄ Music to support the telling of the story in movement

PREPARATION

Set up the chairs and sensory resources ready for sharing the story.

OBJECTIVE

To copy, evaluate and improve a simple sequence of movements.

INTRODUCTION (15 MINUTES)

Cue the lesson using the tambourine and ribbon as usual; you may be able to find ways to introduce a little revision of the previous lesson as you move towards the chairs – perhaps you can include some of the movements the students selected for the story in the previous session.

GROUP TASK (10 MINUTES)

Demonstrate movements in response to stimuli, for example, 'Now I am going to move like a butterfly.' Leave clear room for improvement in your movements and get students to suggest improvements to you. Have them copy your movements and improve them. This lesson is going to be about remembering, copying and improving movements.

INDIVIDUAL/GROUP WORK (20 MINUTES)

The class will now be working in one group or two, depending on whether you have made a whole-class decision on using play-like movements or abstract movements in your representation of the story.

If you have not finished creating movements for the story do this first.

Once you have all the movements for the story, practise them. Split up and watch each other perform the moves, offering feedback and ideas for improvement. Cue the movements using the words from the story, so that the movements happen along with the words.

PLENARY (15 MINUTES)

Run through the improved sequence of movements together. Record the changes that have been made so that you will be able to remember them in the next session. Tell your students that in the next lesson they will have a chance to practise the sequence and then they will perform it for an audience.

Share 'The Selkie Wife' sensory story together.

Lesson plan 6: Rehearsal and performance (1 hour)

This lesson is the culmination of all your students have done so far; it is their chance to show off the movements they have learned to make and to share the story with an audience.

Prior to this lesson you will need to have invited an audience to your performance. It might be that you are able to use this lesson purely for rehearsing and arrange a performance for a time when an audience will naturally be together, for example, an assembly.

RESOURCES YOU WILL NEED FOR THIS LESSON

- ⌃ 'The Selkie Wife' sensory story and associated resources
- ⌃ Chairs

⅄ Music to accompany the performance of 'The Selkie Wife' movement sequence

⅄ Tambourine and ribbon

PREPARATION

Set up the chairs and sensory story resources ready for sharing the story.

OBJECTIVE

To remember and perform a sequence of movements.

INTRODUCTION (15 MINUTES)

Cue the sensory story using the tambourine and ribbon and taking advantage of the opportunity to remind students of particular movements. Share the sensory story together.

GROUP TASK (10 MINUTES)

You have invented and improved movements; now all you have to do is remember them and perform them with control! Run through the movements for the movement sequence together. Stop on any that you feel need to be performed with particular control and spend some time looking at how to do this; you might be giving advice to bend knees slightly to make a standing position more stable or to remember to stretch the fingers as well as the arms to make an extended shape more impressive.

INDIVIDUAL/GROUP WORK (20 MINUTES)

You will probably have time for just one rehearsal. Make the most of it!

Perform 'The Selkie Wife' movement sequence and enjoy the adulation of the crowd.

PLENARY (15 MINUTES)

Look back over all you have achieved over this sequence of lessons. Praise individuals for their personal achievements, and look at how the things that have been learned can be applied elsewhere in life, for example, practising and improving.

Share 'The Selkie Wife' sensory story one final time together.

★

SEASONED WITH SPICE

This story can be sung to the tune of The Searchers' song 'Sugar and Spice'.

Season with spice and all things nice,
Together we will spend this time,
Season with spice and all things nice,
You know our dinner will taste fine.

We all work together to cook our
Dinner in this family.
Be careful 'cause the pots and pans are hot
As they sit upon the stove. You know it is

Seasoned with spice and all things nice,
Together we will spend this time.
Seasoned with spice and all things nice,
You know our dinner will taste fine.

The cutlery clatters as we pass the
Plates around the table.
We chatter and smile as we share our food,
Sitting altogether here. You know it is

Seasoned with spice and all things nice,
Together we will spend this time.
Seasoned with spice and all things nice,
You know our dinner will taste fine.

Everyone around this table loves me,
This is my family.
Sharing food together is a pleasure,
Friendship, laughs and company. You know
   it is

Seasoned with spice and all things nice,
Together we spent this time.
Seasoned with spice and all things nice,
You know our dinner tasted fine.

About the story

Cooking is a very sensory-rich experience – aside from the tastes and smells of food, there are all the sounds of kitchen implements clattering, whisking, blending and boiling, together with the chatter of the family as they ready themselves for sharing a meal. All sensory experiences are valuable, especially to individuals with PMLD, and finding ways to include people with particular needs in those experiences is worth doing. A story like this, which introduces cooking, could be told in the kitchen accustoming the story experiencer to everything that goes on in there so that they could join in again. Perhaps you could even improvise your own songs around things you cook.

John Ockenden, Practice Development Advisor for United Response, (2006) studied how staff in care homes engaged adults with PMLD in activities. Ockenden comments that, 'too many adults with PMLD are sitting around with nothing to do, just because it is not immediately obvious either that they want to be engaged, or how to enable them to be'. One area he identified in particular was cooking; he noted that when there was cooking to be done, the adults with PMLD tended to be left in a different room so that staff members could get on with the task in hand. The staff missed out on an opportunity to provide their clients with the richly stimulating sensory experience. You can use this sensory story/song to introduce cooking to your story experiencer. Because cooking is such a richly stimulating experience, and kitchens themselves can also be rich experiences, some individuals may initially find them overwhelming. By sharing this story in a neutral setting you can build up to sharing it in the kitchen and allowing your story experiencer to become accustomed to everything that is in the kitchen. I hope that in the future you will be able to share cooking as well as stories and songs.

This story/song has been written specifically with blind individuals in mind. It provides rich opportunities to interact via touch, taste and smell. The single visual experience in the story can easily be replaced, for example, with recordings of different people's voices or with objects to touch that represent the different people who would be around the table.

Singing is a very powerful force when it comes to memory. I expect that, no matter how old you are, you will be able to remember a song you sang at school. Singing is great for encouraging people to join in with sound making or vocalisation; it does not matter if you cannot pronounce the words you can still join in. Even those without a voice at all can join in with singing by playing along on musical instruments. Sharing a song unites a group and helps everyone to feel included. The repeating verse will further support those who want to join in but struggle to do so completely.

Try repeating each verse by humming it gently before proceeding to the next verse; this will support the telling of the story in a number of ways.

- ⅄ Humming will help you not to waffle whilst the story experiencer is interacting with the stimuli. (See Chapter 3 for the importance of this.)

- ⅄ Alternating between singing and humming will provide a rhythm to the experience of the story, which will help your story experiencer know what to expect. As you sing they can join in with singing and vocalising. As you hum they can explore the stimuli.

- ⅄ Humming the entire verse before proceeding to the next one will support you in allowing the story experiencer enough time to fully explore the stimuli. It can be tempting to move on quickly from a stimulus, especially a smell. If you remove a stimulus too quickly the story experiencer may not have time to fully process the experience; keeping a stimulus present for the duration of a verse gives the story experiencer a decent amount of time to interact with it, and you can always hum the verse again if you feel they need more time.

Resourcing the stimuli
Shopping list

- ⅄ Fragrant spices (or herbs) – be sure to choose ones that are safe for your story experiencer

- ⅄ Saucepan

- ⅄ Cutlery and plates

- ⅄ Photographs of family members (or objects of reference that relate to them)

Optional

- ⅄ Rice or couscous, cooking apples or chopped tomatoes

Detailed list

Season with spice and all things nice,
Together we will spend this time,
Season with spice and all things nice,
You know our dinner will taste fine.

SMELL, TASTE AND TOUCH

Fragrant spices (or herbs): try to choose spices with a distinctive smell. Be aware that some spices in large quantities can be poisonous or cause skin or eye irritations; also be aware of any allergies your story experiencer may have. Instead of presenting the story experiencer with just the raw spices, you can use them to fragrance something else (see below for ideas). Doing this can be a good way of getting the smell and taste benefits of the spices without risking exposure to too great a quantity of them. Also, having a spiced foodstuff can make it easier for the story experiencer to be able to touch the stimuli. Cooking actions like stirring or rubbing can accentuate the smell experience and are appropriate for these sections of the story.

This stimuli is repeated four times over the course of the sensory song. You may want to encourage your story experiencer to move from smelling, to smelling and touching, to smelling and touching around the face, through to smelling and tasting as the song progresses.

Ideas for spiced dishes:

- ⅄ Cook rice with a little coriander.

- ⅄ Cook couscous in butter with a little garlic.

- ⅄ Heat some chopped tomatoes with a little curry powder.

- ⅄ Stew apples with a little allspice or nutmeg.

- ⅄ You could cook a spiced dish you know or use a shop-bought curry sauce to coat potatoes or rice, etc.

⅄ You can also make sweets with spices in, here is a simple recipe for fudge which you can add spices to; try the following combinations:

    ⅄ White chocolate with vanilla essence.

    ⅄ Dark chocolate with ginger or cinnamon.

    ⅄ Milk chocolate with raisins and nutmeg.

To make the fudge simply melt 500g of chocolate slowly in a pan gently with 400g of condensed milk and 75g of unsalted butter. When the chocolate and the butter have melted, stir in your choice of spices. Pour the mixture into a greased tray and leave in the fridge to cool, you can then cut it into squares and taste it.

Consider whether a dry option, such as rice or couscous will be more suitable to your story experiencer than a wet option such as chopped tomatoes or stewed apples. The wet options might make for a more pleasant taste experience but be off-putting to someone who finds getting their fingers sticky difficult. Consider also whether sweet or savoury will be more appropriate and which will be most likely to engage your audience. Of course, you can opt to have a different experience for each repeat of the 'Seasoned with spice' section – you could imagine that there were different components to the dish and fudge for dessert.

We all work together to cook our
Dinner in this family.
Be careful 'cause the pots and pans are hot
As they sit upon the stove. You know it is

TOUCH

Saucepan: any pot or pan you have around the house will do. Obviously you are not going to present the story experiencer with a pan that is hot from the stove. Warming up the pan by standing it on a hot water bottle, or running it under the hot tap, can give a relevant touch experience of warm metal without being dangerous.

Seasoned with spice and all things nice…

SMELL, TASTE AND TOUCH

As with verse 1.

> *The cutlery clatters as we pass the*
> *Plates around the table.*
> *We chatter and smile as we share our food,*
> *Sitting altogether here. You know it is*

SOUND AND TOUCH

Cutlery and plates: choose a combination that will clatter well – metal knives and forks on plastic plates is a good one.

> *Seasoned with spice and all things nice…*

SMELL, TASTE AND TOUCH

As with verse 1.

> *Everyone around this table loves me,*
> *This is my family.*
> *Sharing food together is a pleasure,*
> *Friendship, laughs and company. You know it is*

SIGHT

Photographs of family members: you can interpret the word 'family' to include all those who care for us as if they were family, so including pictures of friends is appropriate. If you are able to laminate the images they will last longer. If you want to create the feeling of these beloved people being all around, try hanging the images from a curve of cardboard or a bent metal coat hanger so that they can dangle in a semicircle around the story experiencer. Be mindful of where they will be best placed to enable the story experiencer to see them, some experiencers will need to view them closer than others.

> *Seasoned with spice and all things nice...*

SMELL, TASTE AND TOUCH

As with verse 1.

Facilitating the stimuli

Season with spice and all things nice,
Together we will spend this time.
Season with spice and all things nice,
You know our dinner will taste fine.

Offer the story experiencer the spices or spiced rice/couscous mix to smell. Think about how you will present this stimulus – you may choose to use a mixing bowl or something similar that is linked to cooking. Choosing a relatively deep bowl will make it easy for your story experiencer to interact with the stimuli without spilling it. Alternatively, having the stimuli stored in a sealed plastic pot will allow for the air inside the pot to become fragranced and so present a stronger stimulus when opened.

This stimulus repeats four times through the sensory song. You can encourage greater interaction with it on each successive experience. First, your story experiencer may just be sniffing the stimulus; they can then move on to touching it – disturbing the mix may well increase the smell; if it is safe to do so, they can also be encouraged to taste it.

If you have made a spiced rice or couscous mix then presenting it warm is another way of increasing the impact of the smell. If you have made fudge you could present it before it is set, then you would have a fragrant gloopy substance to explore.

We all work together to cook our
Dinner in this family.
Be careful 'cause the pots and pans are hot
As they sit upon the stove. You know it is

Pass your story experiencer a warm pan. Support them in exploring the feeling of the warm metal. Note: Do not use a pan hot from the stove (see the guidance in the detailed shopping list for advice on how to heat the pan safely).

Seasoned with spice and all things nice...

As with verse 1.

The cutlery clatters as we pass the
Plates around the table.

We chatter and smile as we share our food,
Sitting altogether here. You know it is

As long as you have chosen cutlery and plates that will clatter nicely, this stimulus is easy to facilitate. Simply pass the cutlery and plates between you. It does not matter if they get dropped – that will just cause more clattering.

Seasoned with spice and all things nice...

As with verse 1.

Everyone around this table loves me,
This is my family.
Sharing food together is a pleasure,
Friendship, laughs and company. You know it is

Display the images of family and friends at a distance at which the story experiencer will be able to see them easily. If your story experiencer will find a multitude of images difficult to focus on, try presenting them one by one or moving them steadily across their vision.

Seasoned with spice and all things nice...

As with verse 1.

Seasoned with spice and all things nice,
Together we spent this time.
Seasoned with spice and all things nice,
You know our dinner tasted fine.

Exploration activities
Tactile kitchen

Explore how things in the kitchen feel. If you are supporting a deafblind story experiencer you can help them locate items by gently using a hand-under-hand technique to guide them to cupboard doors, drawers, etc.

If you think about a kitchen as a tactile environment, you will very quickly realise what a rich set of sensory experiences it holds: the coldness of metal; the warmth of wooden chopping boards; the stippled nature of plastic chopping boards, graters and even sieves; the grooves in colanders; the shapes of handles, spoons and taps; the wetness of water; the warmth of the oven (be careful of course).

You can add structure to this activity by sorting the different experiences. You could sort kitchen items according to their material: wood, plastic, glass and ceramics. You could create an order of experiences, for example, from bumpy to smooth, or from warm to cool.

Musical kitchen

As anyone who has ever banged a wooden spoon on an upturned saucepan knows, the kitchen is a wonderful source of musical instruments. Rhythm is a very important part of language acquisition, so despite what it may do to your ears, allowing an individual to bang on an improvised drum can be beneficial to their development. If you also bang on something then you can help them to keep the beat.

It does not just have to be drums; exploring the different sounds in the kitchen can be a fascinating experience. These are noises that you probably hear every day and consequently pay little attention to, but if you stop and concentrate on them you can discover a rich auditory environment. Think about: the rattle of cutlery as the drawer is opened; the shiver of a whisk banged against the palm; the squeak of a glass as you rub a damp finger around its rim; the different sounds made by the different materials – making drums of different materials and using different materials as drumsticks; the pops and slurping sounds of lids being removed; the sound of things being cut with knives – vegetables, bread and cheese; the sound of tin foil being torn off a roll; the sound of a tin opener gradually nibbling its way through metal.

To add structure to your sound explorations you can try to create a tune. Filling mugs with different amounts of water and hitting them with a teaspoon can give you melodic notes to accompany your strong rhythm section. If you do not feel you have the musical ability to master a tune, try sound matching activities, for example, what sounds as squeaky as a mouse? What sound is quiet enough to go unnoticed in a library? What sound is as loud as an elephant? Once you have got the hang of this you can begin to create marvellous soundscapes.

A soundscape is not a tune, nor is it a full narrative, but it can tell a story. Think of the way a picture can tell a story. A soundscape is the auditory equivalent of a picture. You could create an eerie soundscape by having shivery sounds (tin foil shaking gently or a hand whisk turning slowly) gradually building up, with a sudden *bang!* at the end. You could create a magical soundscape by having lots of melodic plinking sounds (spoons hitting bottles filled with water, jars of preserves or just against each other) followed by a warm whooshing sound (the sound of the fan oven being turned on) or a happy *ping!* (as the microwave finishes its cycle). Thinking about how the sounds make you feel and deciding whether they are happy or sad sounds can help inform your choices for soundscapes. If you enjoy this activity you could try and build bespoke soundscapes – you could use stories or pictures for inspiration: if someone sends you a postcard can you create a soundscape that suits it. Can you think of a soundscape that would introduce a play of your favourite story? Noticing how sounds are used in TV programmes and films to add interest can help you to hone your soundscaping skills.

Colour and texture exploration

The kitchen can be an artist's playground with so many natural colours and textures available to collage with. Exploring food in a playful way can help children who are reluctant eaters to feel relaxed around it, and, as long as you are using food that does not need cooking, if it happens to get on the fingers and into the mouth whilst you are being creative it does not matter, is not a big deal and can be a very casual way to introduce new flavours and textures to a sensitive palate.

Here are some creative ideas to get you started.

- ⋏ *Foods as paints*: Get a cupcake tray and fill each with a different food substance from the kitchen. Take a paintbrush and a sheet of sugar paper (sugar paper is a good choice as it is very absorbent, but any sort of paper will do) and get painting. You may find diluting some foods makes them easier to paint with. If you want your story experiencer to experience the textures of the foods without them being diluted then using a piece of stiff card and a pallet knife, you can show them how the great oil painters of old often applied their paint to their canvas with a knife.

- ⋏ *Fruit and vegetable portraits*: Have a look at the work of Giuseppe Arcimboldo for inspiration and see if you can lay fruit and vegetables out to look like a human face. Having a soft base to place the fruit and vegetables onto will help you to create your portrait. A section of duvet or a bed of scrunched up newspaper will both provide soft bases and stop your creations from rolling away.

⅄ *Face plates*: Make your lunch look like a face. There are so many different ways to do this and you can have fun creating your own ideas. Here are a few to get you started:

⅄ Eyes: raisins, grapes, small cheese crackers, marshmallows, pepperoni slices.

⅄ Noses: slices of cheese, triangular sandwiches, a carrot with its base cut off sticking straight up off the plate.

⅄ Mouths: red pepper slices, rolled ham, a sprinkled curve of fine grains: a rice mixture, couscous, nuts and seeds, half a round cracker spread with jam.

⅄ Think also of how you might create: cheeks, freckles, moustaches, eyebrows, chins, ears, facial jewellery!

⅄ *Mashed potato landscapes*: Using mashed potato as a base for culinary art can be a very versatile approach. You can sculpt the potato into hills and slopes and add broccoli trees and little huts made of vegetable sticks. Colour the potato with streaks of ketchup or blended peas. Create mosaics with sliced vegetables. Let your imagination run riot.

Creative activities

Family boxes

Create treasure boxes full of information about your family and friends.

PREPARATION

You will need some boxes - shoeboxes are ideal and if you ask in shoe shops they often have spare boxes.

Label the lid of each box with a photograph of a family member. You can label them with a tactile reference, if photos are not useful to you. Wrapping the boxes in different colours of wrapping paper can help to distinguish them - you could get the person in the photograph to choose their favourite wrapping paper from a selection or you could ask them their favourite colour and then wrap the box accordingly.

ACTIVITY

This is an activity to be done over time. If you are supporting someone in creating these boxes it can be nice to put a few things in each box to get them started.

Fill the boxes with things that relate to the person pictured on their lids. Here are some ideas:

- ▲ A dab of their perfume or deodorant on a cotton pad sealed in a plastic pot, for a smell of them.

- ▲ A piece of fabric or an old piece of their clothing washed in their usual laundry detergent.

- ▲ Some of their favourite snacks.

- ▲ A lock of hair.

- ▲ A sample bottle of their favourite shampoo, soap, shower gel or moisturiser.

- ▲ Photos that relate to the person.

- ▲ Items that represent activities you share together, for example, books, balls, pieces from board games.

You can use the boxes as memory boxes and keep things like letters and cards in them, as well as photographs. You could write about activities you have shared together and keep the accounts in the box to come back to at a later date. You might want to find out the same information about everyone, and keep a record. Making an old fashioned set of sorting cards can be a fun way to do this.

Cooking

There are so many things you can cook using herbs and spices. There is a yummy recipe for fudge in the detailed shopping list, and there are many recipes that have herbs and spices amongst their ingredients.

Thinking of cooking as a sensory experience can open you up to creating your own dishes and becoming an intuitive cook. Here is an easy savoury recipe that you can adapt to use various herbs and spices. Have fun exploring different flavour combinations.

YOU WILL NEED

- A large wok

- A wooden spoon

INGREDIENTS

- A dash of olive oil

- A selection of vegetables – try to choose lots of different colours; it will be a healthier meal and look more interesting

- A tin of chopped tomatoes

- Whatever herbs and spices you fancy

METHOD

- Chop the vegetables into thin strips – pieces the length of your little finger and the width of a pencil are perfect.

- Add a dash of oil to the wok and place it on a hot stove.

- Add the vegetables and keep stirring so they do not stick to the bottom. If you have chosen to include onions adding them first can give them lots of time to caramelise, adding a nice sweet taste to the meal. You may choose to add firmer vegetables such as carrots ahead of softer vegetables like peppers.

- If you plan on using fresh spices such as ginger or garlic you can slice them finely and add them during this stage, along with the vegetables.

- Once the vegetables look nearly cooked (onions will become clear, other vegetables might become floppier or change colour slightly, peppers will brown a little), add the tin of chopped tomatoes. Keep stirring until the tomatoes are warmed through and then add your herbs and spices. Add them a little at a time and keep tasting the mixture to see if it tastes good. Be aware that some flavours will change the more they are cooked.

Discovery activities
Nobody's nose!

(My thanks to the Dayton family for introducing me to this game.)
This is a game you can play to find out how well you know your loved ones. It is fun to play at family events, so if you are having a birthday party or having friends round to dinner or a play date, think about setting up a Nobody's nose board.

PREPARATION

Find photographs of all your friends and family and enlarge them using a computer or photocopier, then cut out just the noses. Depending on how hard you want to make the game, add in one or a few noses of people who are not amongst your family and friends; this (or these) noses will be the Nobody's (or Nobodies's) nose (or noses). Mix all the noses up and stick them on a board. Number the noses. Display the board somewhere where everybody will be able to see it.

TO PLAY

The aim of the game is to identify which one of the noses on the board is Nobody's nose.

Allow each person a certain amount of time to look at the board; they can then write down their guess on a slip of paper. Once everyone has had the chance to guess you can reveal your guesses and see who has identified Nobody's nose. For a more gentle pace of play, simply display the board with slips of paper next to it and a box to post answers into. People can view the board at their leisure, write their name and their guess onto a slip of paper and post it into the box. At a suitable point during the day someone can open the box and read out the guesses to discover who has identified Nobody's nose.

EXTENSION

For extra points you can ask people to identify which nose is whose. To help you can provide a list of the names of people whose noses are on display. You might be able to use a nose of a celebrity or public figure as the Nobody's nose to help everyone with their guessing.

VARIATIONS

⅄ *Different body parts*: Try the game using different body parts, what about 'Eye eye!' for identifying whose eyes are pictured? Mouths, eyebrows and even chins can all be interesting parts to identify. If the game is too difficult with just one body part, try pairing them up so that people have a nose and a mouth to go on when they are guessing.

⅄ *Different items*: Try taking photos of people's shoes, coats, scarves, socks or hair, and see if friends and family members can identify each other from these objects.

⅄ *Real items*: Ask everyone attending your party to bring an item with them that they feel represents them. Label each item with a number and play the game in the same way as if you had a board of noses. Alternatively, put all the items into a pillowcase and have the guests at the party pass the pillow case around and each take out an item. Then go around the circle and have each person guess whose object they are holding. You will need to add in a random item that does not belong to anyone in the room – charity shops are a good source of such items. You can theme the items you ask your guests to bring to the party so that you can play the game again and again. Here are some ideas for things to request:

  ⅄ their favourite song

  ⅄ their favourite teddy bear

  ⅄ their best pair of socks

  ⅄ their favourite food

  ⅄ their favourite picture (not photograph)

  ⅄ a sample of their handwriting – you could ask people to write a particular message relating to the party, for example, 'Happy Birthday Nina'.

Plaster of Paris

If you have adventurous family members and friends you might be able to persuade them to allow you to make plaster of Paris models of their body parts. Some body parts are harder to do than others, but hands are an easy place to start.

YOU WILL NEED

- ⊿ Play-Doh

- ⊿ Plaster of Paris

- ⊿ A tub large enough for people to fit their hands into – a large ice cream tub is ideal (and also a great excuse for having to eat lots of ice cream!)

TO MAKE A CAST OF SOMEONE'S HAND

Half fill the tub with Play-Doh. Smooth the Play-Doh out so that it is as level as you can get it. Ask your friend or family member to press their hand firmly into it and then to remove it gently. Check the imprint they have left: does it look like their hand? Have they pressed all their fingers down equally? If it looks okay then it is good to use; if you are not confident then re-smooth the Play-Doh and ask them to try again.

Mix up some plaster of Paris and pour it into the imprint of your friend or family member's hand in the Play-Doh. Do not worry if it goes over the edges in places – as it is in the tub you will not make a mess.

Leave the plaster hand to set. Once it has gone hard you can lift it out of the tub and clean off any bits of Play-Doh that have stuck to it.

Sorting cards

Sorting cards can be used to identify an individual from a set of simple questions. Creating a deck of sorting cards is a good way to stimulate curiosity about our similarities and differences. You can make sorting cards to use as a reference for any group of people or items – for example, a set of sorting cards based on a toy collection, or on possible holiday destinations, or on the professionals you meet in hospital.

PREPARATION

You will need a set of cards that are all the same shape – index cards can be perfect for the job but you may want something larger – pieces of A5 card would be ideal.

Decide what information you want to find out about everyone, for example:

- ⬥ eye colour

- ⬥ hair colour

- ⬥ gender

- ⬥ are they a family member or a friend?

- ⬥ do you know them from home or from school?

- ⬥ are they an adult or a child?

Each item needs to be something that can be phrased as a yes or no question, for example, 'eye colour' could be phrased as, 'Do you have brown eyes?'

Take one index card and punch evenly spaced holes in it down two opposite sides using a hole punch. Leave the top left-hand hole blank; beside each of the other holes write one of your questions.

Punch holes in all the other cards in the same place as the first card.

CREATING THE SORTING CARDS

Take one pre-punched card to interview each family member or friend. Use the card with the questions on as a reference. Write the name of the person who you are interviewing on the new card. If they answer a question with a 'no' cut the hole that relates to that question so that it becomes a notch in the side of the card.

USING THE SORTING CARDS

Once you have made all your cards, you can use them to find out which family members have things in common with each other. Stack all the cards so that they line up nicely. Poke a pencil or stick through the hole that has no question associated with it. Choose a question you wish to ask, for example, 'Who has brown eyes?' Push another pencil or stick through the hole that is associated with that question and lift the deck of cards up. All those people who have brown eyes will stay in the deck supported by two pencils; the people who do not have brown eyes will swing out of the deck and dangle from one pencil only. If you want to ask a combination question, you just need another pencil, for example, you could find out which boys have brown eyes or which people from school have brown eyes.

Grow your own

This activity presents many opportunities for sensory exploration: handling compost, pressing compost into pots, handling herbs, smelling herbs, hearing water pouring, etc.

Making your own garden of herbs and spices will bring you the joy and satisfaction of watching plants grow as well as being a fragrant addition to any room. Cooking with herbs and spices you have grown yourself is more rewarding than cooking with ones bought from the shops and may encourage reluctant eaters to try new flavours.

PREPARATION

Find a large plastic pot with holes in the bottom. If you cannot find a large one you could use several smaller ones. Supermarkets often package fruit and vegetables in plastic pots with holes in the bottom. Stand your pot in a tray on top of several bottle lids. The bottle lids will raise the pot away from the tray a little and allow any excess water to drain out easily. Fill your pots with soil or compost.

GROWING YOUR HERBS AND SPICES

If you have patience then you can grow plants from seeds. Some seeds will grow more quickly than others – cress is a quick grower.

If you want an instant garden, you could go to a garden centre to pick up some small plants. Supermarkets often sell herbs growing in small pots but these are not intended for replanting and may not last long if you try to grow them.

Remember to keep an eye on your plants and keep the soil damp. Placing the pot somewhere where it will get sunlight will help to keep your plants healthy.

It can be nice to choose herbs that produce scent when rubbed gently between the fingers, as then you can experience their aroma without having to deprive the plant of its foliage; herbs like lemon balm and rosemary are good for this.

Concerns about playing with your food

We all know that playing with your food is the gravest flouting of table manners there can be. It is natural that we would worry that allowing children to play with food would encourage bad table manners.

There are two things it is important to consider if you are worried about table manners: your priorities and context.

YOUR PRIORITIES

Playing with food can take away the associated anxiety some children feel about eating. If your story experiencer has difficulties eating, it is likely that it is a higher priority for you that they learn to eat and feel safe and happy doing so, before they learn their table manners. I expect if you had a choice between them having perfect table manners and never being able to eat without experiencing anxiety or being able to eat happily but not doing so in a particularly standard way, you would choose the latter option.

CONTEXT

Context plays an enormous role in behaviour. It is possible to teach an individual that this sort of behaviour is okay in one situation but not in another. If you are worried that playing with food behaviour will carry over into mealtimes, avoid doing playful activities at the dinner table.

If you are sharing these activities with someone who avoids eating or becomes distressed around eating, you may want to create a progression that ends up at the dinner table. First they play with food substances that do not look like food they recognise in a context entirely unrelated to eating. They move along the progression, next playing with food substances that are more recognisable to them as food and in locations more associated with food, until they end up playing with what you hope they will eat for dinner at the dinner table. This can be a very sensible strategy for helping someone to get over their fears surrounding food. If, as soon as you get to the table with real food, you then add in the pressure to behave in a certain way, you inadvertently send messages of anxiety. It is good to allow a period of time where the individual is able to play with their food – and eat it – at the dinner table, before you begin to introduce table manners, so the habit of eating at the table has the chance to become established.

Once you have a person eating happily, you can begin to teach table manners. Table manners are very much a matter of context, for example, eating with our fingers at the table would be frowned upon whereas eating with our fingers at a picnic might not be. Making the person you are teaching aware of the different contexts is the first step. You can support their awareness of context by clearly labelling each situation. You can do this verbally, encouraging them to use the words: inside, outside, table, garden, etc. You can do this through symbols or objects of reference – reinforce the context by presenting the relevant symbol or object at the right time, for example, handing the person a symbol of the table as they go to the table and having a matching symbol on the table where they can place the symbol they are carrying.

Talking about what we do in different places before entering them can help to prepare an individual for the behaviour that will be expected of them once they get there. It also means that any tension that might arise out of the desire to modify behaviour will not be directly associated with the place. You can make this a fun learning game by adding role-play and getting them to copy your actions, for example, present the picture of the table and ask, 'What do we do here?' then answer your own question with actions and encourage the person to join in. Remember to include details that are not related to eating so that it does not become an eating-focused lesson. Things you might do include: say, 'Sit on your bottom,' and then sit down as if on a chair; say, 'Keep your elbows off the table,' and then stick your elbows out to show what elbows are and then pull them back to your ribs; say, 'Use our knife and fork,' and then mime cutting with a knife and lifting food with a fork. You can include things like elbows off the table, as long as joining in feels fun. If this activity is fun then when the individual is at the table they will be able to do these movements and the emotion associated with them will be one of joy (not one of being told off). Difficult tasks like cutting food with a knife can be stressful if they are first encountered alongside being expected to eat a certain quantity of food, so practising these skills through play in other situations can help. Remember that cutting Play-Doh is much easier than cutting food, as you can just apply pressure to a knife instead of a sawing motion. Try to present lots of opportunities to cut different things and learn how to hold them still with a fork whilst sawing with a knife. You can contrast table manners with expected behaviour elsewhere. Choose places where you might eat when exploring behaviour like the park, as well as places you would not eat, like the swimming pool for example.

Six lesson plans for 'Seasoned with Spice'

Since the publication of the new National Curriculum in the UK in 2013, practical cookery lessons have been compulsory for every child up to Year 9 (typically aged 13–14 years). Cookery is not only a fantastic life skill that enhances a child's likelihood of adopting a healthy diet, it is also a great opportunity for a range of sensory experiences. This series of six lessons will help you to revisit the 'Seasoned with Spice' sensory story repeatedly, extending learning on each occasion. This series of lessons focuses on cookery objectives but the story could also be used in other curriculum areas, for example, to support music or PSHE objectives, the activities accompanying the story can be used as tasks in music or PSHE lessons.

Lesson plan 1: Planting herbs and spices (1 hour)

In this lesson students will plant herbs and learn about where fruits and vegetables come from.

If your students enjoy this lesson you might like to explore the free resources provided by Grow Your Own Potatoes.[5]

RESOURCES YOU WILL NEED FOR THIS LESSON

- ⩗ 'Seasoned with Spice' sensory story and associated resources (see page 125 for a list)

- ⩗ Compost or cotton wool and seeds for quick-growing herbs, for example, cress, or small herb plants

- ⩗ Pots to grow your herbs in

- ⩗ A watering can or suitable item for watering plants

- ⩗ A selection of fruit and vegetables – ideally put these in a large bucket with a blanket over the top, or a large cardboard box with a small hole cut in the side, so that children will be able to reach in and feel the items without seeing them

- ⩗ Access to the internet or pre-printed images of the fruit and vegetables you have chosen growing in their natural environments

---

5   These are available by clicking the link to educational resources on my website http://joe.element42.org.

PREPARATION

Make sure you can reach all the resources for the sensory story as you need them. Place the kits to plant herbs on tables around the room where you will send groups to work. Have the internet available (or your pictures ready) and your fruit and vegetables stashed near you.

OBJECTIVE

To gain an understanding of where our food comes from.

INTRODUCTION (15 MINUTES)

Cue the lesson by humming the music to 'Seasoned with Spice'; students and other staff members can join in as they take their seats in the circle. If you are not confident in your humming ability you may be able to find a karaoke version of The Searchers' song 'Sugar and Spice' and play this as your cue.

Share the 'Seasoned with Spice' sensory story with the group. If you have individuals in your group who need the story sharing on a 1:1 basis, have another adult help you – they can provide the stimuli 1:1 to one individual whilst you facilitate it for the rest of the group. Ensure that the adult sharing the stimuli 1:1 with a student knows exactly how to facilitate it for that student and does it in the same way you would do it.

GROUP TASK (10 MINUTES)

This is a movement-based task to energise everyone and to allow any wriggles to come out before the table task.

Explain to your students that our food grows in different places. Make up actions to represent these places, for example, 'under ground' could be to curl up in a ball on the floor, 'on the ground' could be to lie on the ground and 'in a tree' could be to stretch up tall like a tree. You can adapt these actions to suit the different movement needs of your students. Later on in the game you might change what you are looking to identify, for example, switch from looking to spot where something grows to looking to identify which part of it we eat – this could be as simple as saying, 'We eat the insides' or, 'We eat the outsides' and you could run to one side of the room for insides and the other for outsides or jump moving your arms and legs outwards like a star to represent outsides and jump down into a small position on the floor to represent insides.

To play the game each student takes a turn at selecting an item of fruit or a vegetable from the box. Take this opportunity to invite them to explore their senses – what does it feel like? Take it out – what does it smell like? If appropriate, you could let them taste it. They could pass it around the group so everyone gets to experience it.

The cue for the movement will be you saying, 'This is a...! Show me where you think it grows, ready, steady, grow!'

Show an image of the vegetable or fruit growing in its natural environment so everyone can see if they got the answer right. For students with sight impairments, you can speak the answer or offer them a tactile answer, for example, a touch of earth, grass or a stem of a plant (or branch of a tree).

Students who are unable to answer for themselves can experience this activity through their proprioceptive, vestibular and touch senses – first touching the vegetable and then experiencing the movement of their body as they are supported in giving the answer physically.

INDIVIDUAL/GROUP WORK (20 MINUTES)

Students can work on their own or in small groups – whichever suits them best – to plant herbs and spices. Try to enable students to do this as independently as possible, for example, some students may be able to complete the whole task on their own if you give them a simple prompt sheet; others may need physical support to do the planting but will not need telling what to do. Make sure that any adults working to help the students support their independence as well as the task in hand.

Students experiencing this activity on a purely sensory level can be allowed plenty of time to explore the feel of the soil and its smell, as well as the sound of the seeds in their packets and the feeling of them being sprinkled on their skin.

Water the plants once they are planted and explain that everyone will be looking after their plants every day from now on.

PLENARY (15 MINUTES)

Take feedback from the groups about their planting experience. Ask questions about where food comes from – can anyone identify where the components of their favourite meal come from?

Share the 'Seasoned with Spice' sensory story, enjoying calming time together at the end of the session.

Lesson plan 2: Stir-fry vegetables (1 hour)

In this lesson students will select vegetables and cook a healthy meal.

RESOURCES YOU WILL NEED FOR THIS LESSON

- 'Seasoned with Spice' sensory story and associated resources

- A selection of vegetables: onions, leeks, peppers, carrots, broccoli, sweetcorn (perhaps one on the cob and some tinned for ease of use), green beans, red cabbage, etc.

- A tin (or tins) of chopped tomatoes

- Couscous

- A large wok (or woks)

- A cooker (or cookers)

- Knives and chopping boards for cutting up the vegetables

- Olive oil

- A selection of herbs and spices (fresh or dried)

- A colour spinner – you may have one of these in a board game or be able to make one out of a hexagon of card and a sharpened pencil

PREPARATION

Make sure all the resources for the sensory story are easy for you to reach ready for telling the story. Keep the kits for chopping vegetables out of reach until adult supervision is available.

OBJECTIVE

To prepare and cook a healthy, savoury dish.

INTRODUCTION (15 MINUTES)

Cue the sensory story by humming as before, and then share the sensory story as before.

GROUP TASK (10 MINUTES)

Explain to your students that eating a wide range of colours of fruit and vegetables is healthy. Talk to them about the benefit of vegetables in our diets.

Generate an awareness of the different colours of vegetables by playing a movement game in which students must quickly identify the colour of a vegetable:

- ⅄ Clear a space in the room and around the edge of the space place vegetables of different colours, grouping them according to colour.

- ⅄ Ask students to come to the centre of the space and to take it in turns to spin the colour spinner. When the spinner stops turning the student who span it should call out the name of the colour it has settled on. This is the cue for everyone to make their way as quickly as they can to the selection of vegetables of that colour.

- ⅄ When everyone has reached the vegetables you can tell them a little bit about them – what health benefits they offer us, how they are prepared, whether they need to be cooked to be eaten, etc. and then everyone goes back to the centre of the space for the next person's turn.

INDIVIDUAL/GROUP WORK (20 MINUTES)

In groups, or individually, working with minimal support, cook a simple vegetable stir-fry. Adults working to support the groups or individuals should focus their attention on the safety of their chefs and on drawing their attention to the choices they are making.

- ⅄ Choose and chop the vegetables you want in your meal. Chop them into strips about the same size and width as your fingers.

- ⅄ Choose which herbs and spices you will use to season your meal.

- ⅄ Place your wok on a hot hob and add a dash of olive oil. Once the oil is hot add the vegetables. Stir with a wooden implement until the vegetables are cooked (onion will change from opaque to clear and peppers will lose some of their stiffness – as most of the vegetables you are using can be eaten raw, how long you cook them for is a matter of personal preference). Add any fresh herbs you are using.

⬧ Add the tin of chopped tomatoes (you can strain off some of the juice if you think it is too much or that you will not have the time to reduce it). Add your dried herbs and spices.

⬧ Simmer your meal and add the couscous five minutes before the end.

⬧ Wait until it is a comfortable temperature and then tuck in!

PLENARY (15 MINUTES)

Eat what you have cooked together, and discuss what you enjoyed about the cooking process, what you like about the taste of the food and what benefits the vegetables will bring your body. For students who are unable to chew, the mixture can be blended to create a soup. You can have a taste of each other's creations if your friends are willing to share. Students who are unable to swallow can share in the meal by having vegetables touched against their tongue to give them a taste or by smelling the different creations.

To end, share the 'Seasoned with Spice' sensory story together as a group.

Lesson plan 3: Fruit smoothies (1 hour)

In this lesson, students will explore fruit and create a healthy, sweet drink for themselves.

RESOURCES YOU WILL NEED FOR THIS LESSON

⬧ 'Seasoned with Spice' sensory story and accompanying resources

⬧ A selection of fruit and herbs – choose bananas, apples, oranges and other familiar fruit, and also try to also include some more unusual fruits, for example, dragon fruit, kiwi, berries etc.; herbs such as cinnamon and mint can be a nice addition to a smoothie

⬧ A blender

⬧ Bowls to hold chopped fruit

⬧ Cups

⬧ Knives and chopping boards

Optional

- ⅄ Yoghurt and honey

- ⅄ Shot glasses (party shops often sell packs of cheap, plastic shot glasses, you may also find these in the party section of your local supermarket)

PREPARATION
Set up the sensory story resources where you can reach them easily.

OBJECTIVE
To prepare a healthy, sweet drink.

INTRODUCTION (15 MINUTES)
Cue the lesson by humming as before, then share the 'Seasoned with Spice' sensory story as a group.

GROUP TASK (10 MINUTES)
Quickly demonstrate how to chop up some of the fruits on offer in the classroom today. Position the children's chairs in two lines. Students participating in wheelchairs can use these instead of the classroom chairs. Have a bowl for each team near you. Give pairs of children (one child from each team) slices of matching fruit to hold, for example, a child in each team will have a piece of banana to hold, a child in each team will have a slice of apple to hold, etc.

This activity will teach the children that any combination of fruits can be tasty in a smoothie.

- ⅄ Call out the name of a fruit. Students holding this item of fruit have to race to do a whole lap of their line of chairs and sit back down. The person to sit down first is the winner.

- ⅄ Reward the winner by inviting them to add their fruit to their team's bowl of fruit.

- ⅄ Once both teams have at least three items of fruit in their bowl the game ends, and the two bowls of chopped fruit get blended to make a drink for each team.

INDIVIDUAL/GROUP WORK (20 MINUTES)

Working in groups, or individually, choose and prepare fruit to make a smoothie. Take it in turns to use the blender to blend all your fruit into a smoothie. Yoghurt can be added to thicken the smoothie and make it creamier (be alert to any lactose allergies there may be in the group); honey can be added to sweeten (some people think that eating locally sourced honey can help people who suffer from hay fever). Try adding mint to a smoothie made of green fruits or cinnamon to one made with oranges.

Extension/alternative activities: look on the internet for recipes that use fruit and make an alternative product, for example, a fruit salad; freeze your smoothie in lolly or ice cube moulds.

PLENARY (15 MINUTES)

If you have shot glasses you can divide your smoothie up into small portions for students to try. If not, simply pouring a little into normal glasses will work just as well.

Share your smoothies together and discuss what you like about them. Share the 'Seasoned with Spice' sensory story again.

Lesson plan 4: Face plates (1 hour)

In this lesson students will have fun being creative with food.

RESOURCES YOU WILL NEED FOR THIS LESSON

- ▲ 'Seasoned with Spice' sensory story and accompanying resources

- ▲ A selection of healthy food that can be eaten raw – be aware of any allergies your students may have and only use nuts if you are confident that they are safe for everyone

- ▲ A few unhealthy items of food

- ▲ Large, round plates

- ▲ Shopping bags

Optional

- ▲ Blender

- ▲ Pizza bases

- Image of the Eat Well plate showing what a balanced plate of food should look like, which is available from www.nhs.uk/Livewell/Goodfood/Pages/eatwell-plate.aspx – many other variations are available online

- Images of Giuseppe Arcimboldo's portraits

PREPARATION

Set up the resources for the sensory story within easy reach. Place items needed for food preparation on the group work tables together with a plate for each student and Giuseppe Arcimboldo's portraits for inspiration. Set up a shopping experience using the produce you have bought for the lesson.

OBJECTIVE

To make healthy choices and prepare a healthy plate of food.

INTRODUCTION (15 MINUTES)

Cue in the sensory story and share it in the same manner as the preceding lessons.

GROUP TASK (10 MINUTES)

Show the class the Eat Well plate and explain how important it is for us to choose healthy foods to eat. Explain that everyone is going to go shopping and needs to make healthy choices. Give each student a shopping bag and allow them to shop in your 'classroom shop' for the items they will need for the main task.

INDIVIDUAL/GROUP WORK (20 MINUTES)

Look at Giuseppe Arcimboldo's portraits for inspiration. Working in groups, or individually, lay out a plate of healthy food to look like a face. Try to keep to the suggested proportions on the Eat Well plate. Here are a few ideas:

- grated cheese hair

- raisins for pupils and grapes for eyes – if you are really dexterous you may be able to push a raisin into a sliced grape

- sliced meat pink cheeks

⊼ red pepper slice smile

⊼ cucumber nose.

Students who cannot eat solid food can make a smoothie or a soup choosing healthy ingredients.

PLENARY (15 MINUTES)

Share your plates with each other and talk about the choices you made when selecting healthy food. Share the 'Seasoned with Spice' sensory story together.

Lesson plan 5: Herby sandwich (1 hour)

In this lesson students will harvest their crop of home-grown herbs and enjoy eating them in healthy, homemade sandwiches.

RESOURCES YOU WILL NEED FOR THIS LESSON

⊼ 'Seasoned with Spice' sensory story and associated resources

⊼ A choice of breads (try not to use white bread – a seeded loaf and a plain brown loaf would provide two healthy options)

⊼ Sandwich fillings, for example, cheese, sliced meat, salad, etc.

⊼ Your home-grown herbs and spices

⊼ Plates and utensils needed for food preparation

⊼ Large images of different types of food used inside sandwiches

PREPARATION

Lay out the sensory story resources in easy reach. Stack the images of food near your chair. Place a selection of food on each group table along with the utensils they will need to prepare their sandwiches and the plates.

OBJECTIVE

To understand where herbs come from and to use them to create a healthy sandwich.

INTRODUCTION (15 MINUTES)

Cue the session and share the sensory story as usual.

GROUP TASK (10 MINUTES)

The Who's in? game will build your students' awareness of how to create a healthy balance of food in a sandwich. Hand out the large images of sandwich fillings to your students; if you have lots, students can have more than one image.

To play the game you need a sandwich builder and sandwich contents. You can always play the role of the builder if you think your class will find this easier, or you can take it in turns with your students to build the sandwich.

The sandwich builder selects two sandwich contents to build their sandwich with. They then shout out, 'Who's in?' Anyone who thinks that the ingredients they hold would make a good addition to the sandwich can jump up and reply, 'Me!'

The builder then asks the ingredients why they think they should be included in the sandwich. To be included in the sandwich, the ingredients must explain why they would make the sandwich healthier. Having the Eat Well plate you used in the previous lesson for students to refer to can help with this activity.

Once they have built their sandwich, the sandwich builder can pretend to eat it – they do this by using their arms as jaws and their fingers as teeth and munching their way through each ingredient in turn. Ingredients sit down to indicate they have been eaten.

INDIVIDUAL/GROUP WORK (20 MINUTES)

Working individually, or in small groups, prepare healthy sandwiches – choose and harvest herbs to add to the sandwiches.

Adults working with the groups can support them in the safe use of utensils and give them extra information to enable them to make the healthiest choices.

PLENARY (15 MINUTES)

Look at each other's sandwiches and talk about why they are healthy and make suggestions as to how they could be made even healthier. Talk about how the herbs grew and what grows outside - notice that different things grow at different times of year and that the herbs taste particularly good because they are fresh. Link this to an understanding that produce will be at its best when it is in season.

Share the 'Seasoned with Spice' sensory story again together.

Lesson plan 6: Fudge frolics (1 hour)

In this lesson students will explore spices and prepare and enjoy homemade fudge.

RESOURCES YOU WILL NEED FOR THIS LESSON

- 'Seasoned with Spice' sensory story and associated resources
- Ingredients for making fudge (see page 127)
- Images of various fruits and vegetables
- A selection of blended fruits and vegetables
- Herbs and spices
- A box with a blanket over the top with various fruits and vegetables hidden inside
- Small chunks of fruit or vegetables

PREPARATION

Make sure the resources for the sensory story are within easy reach. Place the images of fruit and vegetables on one table, the selection of blended fruits and vegetables together with the herbs and spices on a second table, the box with fruit and vegetables hidden inside on a third table and on the final table lay out the small chunks of fruit and vegetables.

OBJECTIVE

To make decisions about how to season a dish based on an appreciation of taste, smell and texture.

INTRODUCTION (15 MINUTES)

Cue in the lesson and share the sensory story as usual.

GROUP TASK (10 MINUTES)

Invite your students to take part in a sensory exploration carousel. Allocate a few students to each of the four tables. Once at a table the students should explore what is on offer using the relevant sense: sight, taste, touch and smell. Their challenge is to identify the fruit and vegetables. After a couple of minutes everyone moves around one space on the carousel and explores the next table. This continues until everyone has visited all four tables. Talk about which experiences you liked the best.

INDIVIDUAL/GROUP WORK (20 MINUTES)

Working individually or in small groups, make the fudge as described on page 127. Focus on making thoughtful choices about flavourings for the fudge. Adults supporting the students can help them to explore the possible flavour combinations – smelling and tasting the possible flavours is a good way of doing this.

PLENARY (15 MINUTES)

Enjoy and share your fudge. Talk about the seasoning choices you made. Recognise that sweet foods like fudge can be a part of a healthy diet, as long as you do not eat too much of them!

Share the 'Seasoned with Spice' sensory story together.

★

TWO PEOPLE MADE ME

*One egg from Mummy and one sperm from
   Daddy and there I was! One cell dividing
   and growing inside Mummy's womb.*

*My heart began to beat and my eyes grew,
   though I kept them closed.*

*I grew fingers and toes, I swam and I kicked.
   My skin was covered with soft lanugo fur.*

*As my ears developed I began to hear
   sounds from outside the womb.*

*Mummy ate for me. I could taste bitter and
   sweet.*

*The bigger I grew the more squashed I
   became. On my birthday Mummy and I
   worked hard to bring me into the world.*

*And then I was here! Able to stretch out,
   see, smell, touch, taste and hear: ready to
   explore the world.*

About the story

Pregnancy can be a mysterious time; from the outside we watch a bump grow. A mother-to-be may feel her baby move; she will feel her body change and grow to support her baby, but what is going on inside the womb is hidden. Developments in science and human understanding can now tell us what is happening inside the womb at every stage of pregnancy: we know when a foetus first opens its mouth and tastes the amniotic waters in which it swims; we know when its fingers and toes form; we know when it begins to hear.

Each one of us was once inside a bump, and knowing about this very early part of our lives can be fascinating. We may have had the experience of watching a bump grow and waiting to meet our child, our sibling or a new friend, and knowing about their development as they grow can help us to get to know them before they are born.

Many people have journeys to pregnancy and birth that are different in some way to the one described here. Change the words of the story to suit your personal journey, for example, you may want to add that doctors and nurses worked hard to bring your child into the world, or you could say Mummy's egg and a sperm if conception was a result of sperm donation. You may also want to adapt the final line of the story to reflect the capabilities your child has, for example, replacing seeing with giggling and resourcing this with a tickle instead of a sight experience. Personalising the story will make it a more powerful experience for your story experiencer.

Resourcing the stimuli
Shopping list

- A single ball
- A drum (or sturdy cardboard box)
- Fur fabric or velvet
- A large, cardboard take away cup (the perfect excuse to treat yourself to a drink when you are shopping)
- Lemon juice
- Honey

    ⅄ A large scarf or sheet

    ⅄ Your choice for multiple sensory stimuli – see detailed list

Detailed list

> *One egg from Mummy and one sperm from Daddy and there I was!*
> *One cell dividing and growing inside Mummy's womb.*

TOUCH

Understanding the concept of oneness is actually quite hard to do. Before we are able to count we need to have had experiences of one and many. The repeated use of the word 'one' in this phrase is a good opportunity to reinforce a link between a single item and the word 'one'. It is useful if you can choose an item that does not already have its own connotations in the mind of your story experiencer, for example, do not use their favourite toy or an item familiar to them by a different name. A single ball would be a simple way of handing your story experiencer an experience of oneness.

You may be able to highlight further the oneness of the item you present to the story experiencer by having many others present, for example, lifting one marble from a bag of marbles gives the experience of one and of many. (Do not use marbles with individuals who are liable to swallow them.)

> *My heart began to beat and my eyes grew, though I kept them closed.*

SOUND

The ability to keep a beat is a better indicator of later language skills than even a mother's educational background. Rhythm is such an important part of language, and an understanding of rhythm helps us to speak, listen and even read. Our mother's heartbeat is the first beat we encounter, and the beat of a human heart is a very evocative sound to any one of us.

You may be able to find a recording of a heartbeat on the internet to play to illustrate this section of the story, or you may choose to create a beat yourself. Try to choose a deep drum or a large box that will produce a gentle sound rather than a sharp tap. You may be able to alter the sound slightly by adding a muffling element such as a piece of fabric either inside or over the drum. Keep a steady beat to indicate the mother's heartbeat. Allow your story experiencer to join in with creating the beat with you. You can hold their hand to support them in co-creating the beat with you or simply allow them to share the drum with you and beat a rhythm alongside you.

> *I grew fingers and toes, I swam and I kicked. My skin was covered with soft lanugo fur.*

You can choose to illustrate this section of the story with movement or touch.

MOVEMENT

Early on in the womb a baby has a lot of space to swim around and move about. Later in pregnancy their limbs will be curled up to fit inside the relatively small space of the womb, but at nine weeks they are smaller than a little lime and are free to wriggle about in the space. Our proprioceptive sense tells us where our body is in space and our vestibular sense informs us about movement and balance – you can use these senses to illustrate this section of the story by allowing/encouraging/supporting your story experiencer to move around in a space as if they were a foetus moving in the space of a womb.

TOUCH

Babies in the womb pass through lots of different stages, for example, when they first grow they have a tail and webbed toes and fingers! One of these stages is fur. Yes, a baby in the womb will be covered with a soft fur called lanugo fur. This has vanished before a baby is born, but it is fun to think of all the changes a baby has been through before it enters the world. You can illustrate this section of the story with a touch experience of soft downy fur – choose a suitable fur fabric or a long pile velvet to provide the experience.

> *As my ears developed I began to hear sounds from outside the womb.*

SOUND

We can only imagine what noises from outside the womb must sound like to a baby inside the womb. If you have ever put your head underwater at a swimming pool and listened to a conversation going on at the side of the pool you have had the experience of hearing sound made outside of water from within water. It is this sort of distortion of sound that you are looking to create with this stimulus. I have two suggestions as to how you might create the impression of sound being listened to from within water; try them out on yourself or a friend first before sharing them with your story experiencer.

- ▲ *Using just your hands*: Place the flats of your hands against the story experiencer's ears and press just hard enough to bend the soft parts of the ear but not so hard that you clamp your hands to the side of their head. As you speak, gently move your hands in small circles or up and down movements. This will create a sibilant sound in competition with your own voice.

- ▲ *Using a cardboard cup*: Seal your mouth inside the cardboard cup by pressing it into the soft flesh of your cheek, upper lip and chin. When you speak into the cup your voice will be muted and unclear.

Mummy ate for me. I could taste bitter and sweet.

TASTE

A baby's mouth and tongue are one of the first facial features to become operational. A baby in the womb will open its mouth at around ten weeks; inside will be a tiny tongue and the baby can take sips of the amniotic fluid. The baby will taste some of the flavours that the mother is eating, for example, if she eats a lot of spicy foods the baby will become familiar with those flavours. Bitter and sweet tastes are easiest for the baby to distinguish.

You can facilitate bitter and sweet tastes using lemon juice and honey; these can be dripped onto the tongue. If your story experiencer is able to facilitate tastes themselves then offering them a slice of lemon and a sweet such as a marshmallow will be an easy way of providing them with bitter and sweet taste experiences.

The bigger I grew the more squashed I became. On my birthday Mummy and I worked hard to bring me into the world.

TOUCH

During the later stages of pregnancy, the baby does not have as much space to move around inside the womb. It will still stretch and kick but to do so it will have to push against the mother; if you are watching the bump you may see it move as a little foot sticks out and the baby inside has a wriggle. Prior to birth, a baby will be very confined by the womb; its arms and legs will be bent up and curled against its body. You can create this confined feeling for your story experiencer by wrapping them tightly in a piece of fabric – a large scarf or a sheet would be ideal. Your story experiencer can push against this wrapping like a baby kicking in the womb or pushing its way out into the world.

> *And then I was here! Able to stretch out, see, smell, touch, taste and hear: ready to explore the world.*

MULTI-SENSORY!

If you feel that multiple experiences might overwhelm your story experiencer then use the movement of stretching to illustrate this section of the story. If you want to go for the whole caboodle try providing sight, smell, touch, taste and sound experiences – you could choose ones that are associated with the first moments of life, personal favourites for your story experiencer or a set of strong experiences aimed at invigorating each sense in turn. Here are some suggestions.

- *Sight*: A kaleidoscope, scraps of coloured metallic paper showered in front of the story experiencer's eyes, a rainbow filter on a projection wheel.

- *Smell*: A hot flavoured drink with a sweet aroma such as hot blackcurrant, a zingy scented essential oil on a cotton pad, a spritz of perfume.

- *Touch*: A texture board with a variety of textures attached, a string of knobbly objects, a bucket filled with differently textured items such as a wet sponge at the bottom with shredded paper above it hiding other interesting tactile objects.

- *Taste*: Milk, water, favourite foods or drinks.

- *Sound*: Welcoming words such as 'Hello', the crying of an infant, a big noise like a trumpet fanfare or crash of symbols, entrance music, happy birthday song.

Facilitating the stimuli

One egg from Mummy and one sperm from Daddy and there I was!
One cell dividing and growing inside Mummy's womb.

Pass the single object to your story experiencer and allow them time to experience it.

My heart began to beat and my eyes grew, though I kept them closed.

Produce the rhythm of a heartbeat using a drum or sonorous cardboard box. If your story experiencer is likely to experience the sound in a passive way, consider where you will be best placed to create the sound – will they be more responsive if they can see your movements? Will they be more responsive if the sound is louder or closer to them? Watch for indications that they are responding to the rhythm – we naturally tap our feet or hands to a beat so try to spot if they begin to produce rhythmic movements.

If your story experiencer is able to co-create the beat or cooperate with creating the beat then allow this to happen. Co-creators can share the drum with you and try to match their beats to yours. If they cooperate, you may be able to help them to create the beat themselves by supporting their arm (or leg – they can make the beat with any part of their body). They may allow you to use their hand to create the beat. Another option can be to create the beat on something on which they can rest their hand (or foot or other body part), for example, you could use the flat of your palm to create a beat on a lap tray on which they could also rest their hand. They may be able to rest their hand on the drum as you produce the beat. Simply resting the drum in their lap can amplify the experience for them, as they will hear the sound and feel the vibrations of the beat as it is produced.

I grew fingers and toes, I swam and I kicked. My skin was covered with soft lanugo fur.

MOVEMENT

Movement can be anything you like – whatever suits you. You might help your story experiencer to move their limbs; you might be able to move them around using a wheelchair and explore the space in the room where you are sharing the story. For more able story experiencers you could encourage them to make the movements they think a baby might make in the womb.

TOUCH

Present the fur fabric or velvet against something that will make it easier to feel the pile. Simply handing over a bundle of fabric will not give the sensation of stroking soft fur. Attaching the fabric to a stiff piece of card or wrapping it around a cushion will allow the story experiencer to be able to stroke it and feel its softness. Remember a touch does not have to be experienced with the hands – feet and faces are also good at touching. If your story experiencer is passive you can stroke the fabric against their skin to allow them to feel it. A single stroke of the fabric may not be enough for your story experiencer to take on-board the experience; allow the time for the sensation to be fully appreciated. Be watchful for the story experiencer's reactions and stop if they appear to dislike the sensation.

As my ears developed I began to hear sounds from outside the womb.

Choose which method of sound distortion you plan to use with your story experiencer. Think about their preferences when making this decision: will they be distracted or upset by you touching their ears? Is their hearing impaired – will they be able to hear the muted sounds produced by speaking into a cup?

Speak words that you would typically hear around the house or words that someone talking to a bump might use, for example, 'Hello in there, how are you? We cannot wait to meet you.' Decide on what these words will be and make a note of them so that you are able to deliver this sound stimulus in the same way each time you share the story.

Mummy ate for me. I could taste bitter and sweet.

You can offer bitter and sweet taste experiences for your story experiencer to try. Present the foods or liquids in a way that suits your experiencer, for example, in a cup that they will be able to hold or by flavouring mashed potato (which does not fall off spoons easily) with lemon juice or honey.

If your story experiencer is unable to eat, you can still present taste experiences by using a pipette to drip a small amount of fluid onto the tongue (just enough so that the tongue is coated). You can create a bitter solution by adding lemon juice to water and a sweet solution by mixing honey and water. Be aware of any allergies your story experiencer may have and choose your experience accordingly.

> *The bigger I grew the more squashed I became. On my birthday Mummy and I worked hard to bring me into the world.*

A baby's limbs are all bundled up inside the womb prior to birth; you can facilitate the same sensation for your story experiencer by swaddling them in cloth. A large scarf such as a pashmina, sheet or blanket would do. Do not cover your story experiencer's face or apply pressure anywhere that could hurt them. Be aware of your story experiencer's breathing; your aim is to create a confined feeling not bind them so tightly that it restricts their breathing. If you do not have a blanket or scarf to hand you might be able to create the same effect using their clothes and just pinching up a little of the fabric in your hand so that the garment is more restrictive.

> *And then I was here! Able to stretch out, see, smell, touch, taste and hear: ready to explore the world.*

This final section of the story can be facilitated using the movement of stretching or through exploring all of your senses in sequence. To facilitate it supported by movement you can stretch yourself and indicate for your story experiencer to copy you, or you can support them physically to extend their limbs in a stretch.

Illustrating this section of the story using multiple stimuli will mean you need to be quite well organised in order to deliver the stimuli smoothly in succession. What you do will depend on the stimuli and your story experiencer. Here is an example:

1. *Sight*: Throw a fist full of coloured paper into the air in front of your story experiencer (then reach for the perfume).

2. *Smell*: Mist the air above your story experiencer with perfume so that it follows the coloured paper as it falls.

3. *Touch*: Lift a texture board so that it sits on your story experiencer's lap and support them in exploring the different textures.

4. *Taste*: Remove the texture board and offer your story experiencer their favourite snack.

5. *Sound*: Sing happy birthday as they finish eating their snack.

Having so many stimuli happen one after another can be overwhelming for some story experiencers. You will know if it is too much for your story experiencer. If you feel that it is then simply illustrating this section with the stretch movement is an easy alternative, or you may opt to pick just a few stimuli or present weakened versions of the various experiences, for example, a multi-coloured sheet of paper, a smell wafted under the nose, a simple touch of their hand, a sip of water and a gentle tune.

The story ends with the individual ready to explore the world. If you have an activity planned for after the sensory story this can be a great cue to start it. Suggestions for activities can be found in the next section.

Exploration activity
Baby world

When the baby is born it sets about discovering the world using all of its senses; you can choose any sensory experience to form a part of this discovery! However, you might like to think about the sorts of experiences a baby is first likely to encounter – baby clothes, baby lotion, baby powder, baby toys including those with rattles and flashing lights, baby food and the sound of lullabies or perhaps the vacuum cleaner. Your story experiencer can take on the role of the newborn child and experience different scents, tastes, textures, sounds and sights of their new world. You can structure these experiences by presenting a narrative of a baby's day: waking up, hearing their mother, being dressed, eating, playing with toys, being washed, and so on.

Creative activities
Fingers and toes

In the third section of this story the baby's fingers and toes become distinct; until this point in its development a baby's fingers and toes are webbed.

If your story experiencer is physically able to, they can explore their fingers and toes by setting them challenges.

- ↟ *Finger challenge*: Balance a penny on the pad of your thumb and pass it to your index finger without using your other hand. If the penny began with heads facing up then it must end up with tails facing up on your index finger. Then pass it from your index finger to your middle finger, again making sure it turns over, so this time it would be heads up. Continue until it rests on your little finger.

⋏ *Toe challenge*: Can you lift up and put down each toe in turn moving only one toe at a time?

If you are not ready for these very difficult challenges yet then you can challenge your fingers and toes with other tasks, for example, lifting things up or drawing in lines.

You can use finger painting and toe painting to have fun exploring your fingers and toes. If you cannot move your fingers and toes yourself you can have help to do so. Here are a few ideas of things you could paint with your fingers (or toes).

FINGER PAINTING IDEAS

⋏ *Flowers*: Use your fingerprints to create the petals of flowers. Add green stems and leaves to your drawing using a felt-tip pen once the paint has dried. Try using fingerprints to paint grape hyacinths – draw a long stem with a green felt-tip pen, dip your fingers into blue paint and print all the way up the stem on both sides.

⋏ *Trees*: Draw a tree trunk and branches using a brown felt-tip pen. Use your fingerprints, or toe prints to add green leaves to the tree.

⋏ *Christmas decorations*: Use black card or paper as a background for your painting. With a pale-coloured drawing pencil draw the outlines of a street and houses. Draw zigzag lines between the houses to hang your Christmas lights from. Choose lots of different colours and fingerprint along the lines to be the Christmas lights hanging in the street. You could use the same technique on green card to decorate a Christmas tree with coloured lights.

Healthy eating

When a woman is pregnant it is very important that she eats a healthy diet, as what she is eating will be nourishing both her and the baby. Different foods help our body in different ways. Here is a song you can sing to boost awareness of healthy eating. You can add your own verses to the song. It is very simple – you sing it to the tune of 'Frère Jacques' and the lines repeat so one person can sing them and another copy them. Try eating small amounts of the things mentioned in the song just after each verse.

Healthy eating,
          Healthy eating,
Is good for you,
          Is good for you,
Drink lots of water,
          Drink lots of water,
To keep hydrated,
          To keep hydrated.

Healthy eating,
          Healthy eating,
Is good for you,
          Is good for you,
Eat some oily fish,
          Eat some oily fish,
To help your brain,
          To help your brain.

Healthy eating,
          Healthy eating,
Is good for you,
          Is good for you,
Eat lots of vegetables,
          Eat lots of vegetables,
To get vitamins,
          To get vitamins.

Healthy eating,
          Healthy eating,
Is good for you,
          Is good for you,
Eat some juicy oranges,
          Eat some juicy oranges,
To keep colds away,
          To keep colds away.

Make up your own verses. It is easy to do.

Discovery activities
Dividing cells

The story starts with a single cell, which divides. It divides into two cells, which in turn grow and divide into two cells each, making four cells. The four cells become eight, the eight become sixteen, sixteen become thirty-two and so on. This can be hard to picture in our imaginations and very difficult to watch because the cells themselves are very small and hidden away. However, you can create a representation of this using washing-up liquid and a straw. Extra strong bubble mixture will work even better than washing-up liquid. The small straws on the sides of drinks cartons that have diagonally cut ends are also useful when doing this. Here are how to do it.

- ⅄ Prepare a clean, flat surface that will be easy for everyone to see. The surface needs to be smooth and must be one you do not mind getting washing-up liquid on.

- ⅄ Dip the end of your straw into the washing-up liquid and blow a single bubble onto the flat surface and say, 'This is the one cell.'

- ⅄ By keeping your straw inside the bubble you can blow gently to make it grow. Say, 'The cell grows.'

- ⅄ Remove your straw from the bubble and place it so that its end is in contact with the flat surface on one side of the bubble; draw it smoothly straight through the bubble. This will cut the bubble into two linked bubbles. Say, 'The cell grows and then divides, forming two cells.'

- ⅄ If you have the small, diagonally cut straw, quickly (as bubbles have a limited shelf life) insert the sharp end of the straw into one of the two bubbles and blow gently a little bit, then repeat with the other bubble. Say, 'The two cells grow.'

- ⅄ Remove your straw and place it so that its end is in contact with the flat surface, but this time make sure that when you draw it smoothly through the bubbles it will pass through both, cutting them into four. Say, 'The cells grow and divide.'

- ⅄ As quickly as you can, repeat the process, but this time you will have to draw the straw through the bubbles twice to chop the four bubbles into eight. You can continue doing this for as long as your bubble mixture or washing-up liquid holds out.

Adding a few drops of food colouring can make the bubbles easier to see. If you have access to an overhead projector then blowing the bubbles on the glass mirror of the projector will allow you to project them onto a wall making it possible for lots of people to see at once.

Number sequences

It can be fun to explore the sequence of numbers the dividing creates. One way of doing this is by using modelling clay.

Begin by giving your story experiencer a small ball of clay, and ask them to divide it in two. Give them a little bit more clay to add to the two pieces of clay they now have and get them to roll the new clay into the existing clay to grow the two balls. You can help them to manipulate the clay. As you are doing this you can explain the first section of the story in more detail:

'First there was just one cell.' Hand the story experiencer one small ball of clay and give them the time to feel it with their hands.

'That cell divided.' Support your story experiencer in pulling the small ball of clay apart into two pieces.

'Now there are two.' Count the two pieces of clay with your story experiencer.

'Each cell grew.' Add a little clay to each of the two existing pieces. Help your story experiencer to roll the new clay into the old to create two separate balls.

'The two cells…' Count the two balls together…

'…both divided.' Support your story experiencer in pulling apart the two balls of clay to form four pieces of clay.

Continue in the same way until your run out of clay!

Although this story is well known, people experiencing it for the first time can find it amusing that the cells just keep on dividing. They can share this sense of fun with you as you share the exploration with them.

You can further support your exploration by writing down the numbers you discover or by colouring them in on a hundred square.

You can explore the number sequence in other ways, for example, painting dots to represent the cells as they grow and divide. How many times will they be able to divide before there is no longer room on your page? You could use marbles or unit cubes to lay out the sequence, beginning with one, then two cubes, then four and so on until you run out.

More cognitively able story experiencers may enjoy discussing how these cells come to form the different parts of the body. Looking at pictures of different types of cells can be very interesting: think about nerve cells – they look like little fireworks going off; red blood cells have a dimple in them for carrying oxygen; muscle cells are long and stretchy. You can show your story experiencer the different pictures of cells and ask them to guess which one does which job; this is a good way to get them thinking about the reasons why the cells are different shapes. Could they invent a cell for a particular job? Or draw what they think a particular type of cell might look like? If you are able to get a microscope you can show them the cells in an onion by peeling off a single layer of onionskin and looking at it through the microscope.

Keep the beat

Being able to join in with and keep a beat is an important part of the development of communication. Sharing in creating a beat is a bonding experience, and many cultures use collective drumming as part of traditional rituals.

You can explore the second section of this story together with your story experiencer further by sharing beats together. Add interest by creating beats using different things – lots of things you can find around the house will lend themselves to becoming percussion instruments, with a little imagination. It can also be fun to use different parts of the body to keep rhythm: tapping your feet, clapping your hands, slapping your thigh or tapping your cheek whilst holding your mouth open. Using the body can add a tactile experience to this auditory one, which your story experiencer may enjoy.

You can develop the idea of the heartbeat by listening to your own heartbeat. If you happen to have a stethoscope, that's fantastic, but if not you may find that even a child's plastic toy stethoscope will allow you to hear a heartbeat. Feeling your heartbeat either by placing your hand on your chest or taking your pulse is interesting to learners.

Once you have identified your heartbeat, you can try to produce a beat to match it. You can develop this activity by seeing if you can mimic other animals' heartbeats. Little birds and mice have fantastically fast heartbeats, whereas some larger animals like horses and whales have much slower heartbeats. A blue whale's heart beats only six times a minute. The next activity shows how you can make a game of this exploration.

That is my beat
PREPARATION

- Print out pictures of different animals from the internet (or use postcards or photographs).

- Look up the heart rates for the different animals and write these on the back of the pictures.

- Try to choose animals with a range of different heartbeats, from the very high to the very low.

OPTIONAL EXTRA

Create a heartbeat scale by writing in a continuous line the numbers from zero to the highest heart rate you have for an animal in your set of cards. Divide the line of numbers up into sections and label these according to the speed of the heart rates indicated within the sections, for example, slow, fast, very slow, very fast, etc.

TO PLAY THE GAME

- Choose a card and hand it to your partner without looking at the back of the card.

- Your partner looks at the back of the card, so that they know the heartbeats per minute of the animal you have chosen but you do not.

- Create what you think the heartbeat of the animal would sound like using any instrument you want.

- Your partner can tell you whether you are right or wrong or conduct you to increase or decrease your speed.

- If you get the heart rate right, you keep the card with the animal on it. If you fail to get the heart rate right then the card is discarded.

- Swap roles – now your partner chooses a card and gives it to you to look at. They create the beat and you tell them if they have got it right or wrong. At the end of their go, award them the card or discard it.

⌃ Continue to take turns until there are no cards left.

⌃ The winner is the person who has collected the most animal cards.

ALTERNATIVE VERSION

⌃ Choose two animal cards and read their heart rates. Do not show their heart rates to your partner. Place the cards in front of you and begin to play the beat that matches the heart rate of one of the animals on your cards.

⌃ Your partner must guess which animal's heart rate you are mimicking. If they get it right they keep the animal card; if they get it wrong you keep the card. The other card is discarded.

⌃ Take it in turns to be the person guessing until you are out of cards.

You can make this game harder by having more animals for your partner to guess from, for example by choosing three animals at the start. If you choose larger numbers of cards you may decide to allow your partner more than one guess, for example, if you are laying out five cards you might allow your partner two guesses to identify your animal. If you are using large numbers of animals to guess between, instead of discarding the cards that were not chosen, put them back into the main pack (otherwise you will run out of animals too quickly).

Six lesson plans for 'Two People Made Me'

In this series of lessons students will explore the gestation period of a baby in the womb by asking questions and using their own experiences as well as second-hand sources to find out the answers to these questions. The lessons are based around science objectives but there is clear scope for extending learning into PSHE and also for learning about what happens before and after this phase of life.

Over the course of these lessons students will contribute to a classroom display, which will provide them with a place for exploring and reflecting on their learning at other times.

Lesson plan 1: Where do babies grow? (1 hour)

In this lesson students will come to understand that before being born, a baby grows inside a woman's womb. They will make links with personal experiences to understand that this is an experience common to all people.

RESOURCES YOU WILL NEED FOR THIS LESSON

- 'Two People Made Me' sensory story and associated resources

- A diverse range of images of pregnant women – try to include images of women from different cultures, women of different ages, women of different abilities and women at different stages of pregnancy

- Photographs of pregnant women known to your students – these could be photographs of a teacher in the school who has been pregnant, photographs of the students' mothers when they were pregnant with the students or with their siblings or other people known to your students, for example, care workers, friends of the family or members of the local community

- A selection of small and large items

- Paper, drawing materials and scissors for students to use

- Modelling clay for students who are not able to draw

- All of the lessons in this series will be cued in by the smell of a product typically used in the care of babies. Choose something that will be safe to use with everyone in your class, for example, baby lotion or talcum powder. Decide how you will share this cue with them – you might create a puff of talcum powder in one place in the room and allow the smell to disperse gradually or you might put a drop of baby lotion into each student's palm and allow them to rub it in and smell its aroma.

RESOURCES AND PREPARATION FOR THE CLASS DISPLAY

You will need a large paper cut-out of a woman's mid-section displayed on a classroom notice board (you can use an image of a whole woman if you have space on your notice board, but the abdomen will need to be large enough to fit a sheet of A3 paper within it). This woman is going to have a special adaptation to her tummy to allow us to see inside, so make a 'lift the flap' extra tummy and lower abdomen and staple this so that it can be easily lifted. If you have sticky-backed Velcro you can put tabs on the notice board so that the flap can be lifted and held open whilst people look inside. Leave space around the woman for students' work and photographs to be added later.

If you have small whiteboards and can attach two of these to your notice board, that's great. If not, you can use paper. These will be used to indicate what month of pregnancy your display woman is in and what she looks like in profile i.e. how big her bump is!

PREPARATION

Place the resources for telling the sensory story so that they are easy for you to reach as you share the story with your students.

Prepare the display board and images of foetal development as described above.

OBJECTIVE

To use personal experience to answer scientific questions.

INTRODUCTION (15 MINUTES)

Cue the lesson using whichever baby product you have chosen. Share the 'Two People Made Me' sensory story with the class.

GROUP TASK (10 MINUTES)

This task is called Small and Big. Ask your students to divide up your selection of items into small and big items. You can do this as a whole class, in a mad scramble: just dump the items on the floor and ask students to place all the large items on a table and all the small items on a chair as quickly as they can. Or you can be a little more organised about it and give items to each child and take turns to say whether the item you have is small or big before placing it in the appropriate pile. Or you can add a challenge and ask the class to arrange the items in order from small to big.

Once you have your items divided, ask your students which pile, or where in the line, some other items would go, for example, the school building, a single pea, a grain of sand and the school bus.

Allow students who are unable to sort the items to experience small and big items through touch and sight.

INDIVIDUAL/GROUP WORK (20 MINUTES)

Explain to your students that when a baby begins to grow it is very small.

Tell your students that their task in this lesson is to work out where a baby grows. You can give some silly suggestions for answers. Is it on a tree? Is it in a shop? Do not take their answer now; they must show you where it grows. There are two stages to this answer, the first is to recognise that a baby grows inside a woman, and the second is to be able to say where inside a woman.

Students can look at the images you have supplied and any photos they have brought into class themselves and record their answer to the question, 'Where does a baby grow?' They can record their answer in writing, by drawing, using a computer, verbally, using sign language or gesture or in any other way that suits them.

Once students have completed part one of their answer, draw their attention to the large cut-out of a woman on the classroom wall. Remind them that when a baby is first inside a woman it is very small – only a few cells. Set them the task of creating a small baby to go inside the woman on the wall. Provide them with the resources they will need to do this, for example, paper, drawing equipment and scissors.

Adults working to support the students during this time should take the opportunity to engage the students in conversation about what they understand about development and their own experiences of pregnant women. The tasks themselves do not take much time to do, doing them provides the opportunity for discussion.

Students who are not able to draw can use clay to make small and large shapes. Encountering the difference between small and large is a scientific step along the way to understanding growth.

PLENARY (15 MINUTES)

Look at the paper babies your students have created. Choose one to add to your display, and place it low down in the woman's abdomen where the womb would usually be (it only moves out of the groin area in the second trimester of pregnancy, i.e. when a woman is over three months pregnant).

Share the sensory story 'Two People Made Me' to end the lesson.

Lesson plan 2: How do babies grow? (1 hour)

This lesson will introduce students to the stages of development a baby goes through in the womb. Students will recognise that growing involves something getting bigger and that changes occur as we grow.

Show them the series of images you have of foetal development and tell them that the lady on the wall is going to get more pregnant as this series of lessons progresses. Show them the pictures of the embryo at the early stages of pregnancy and explain that generally a woman does not get a bump until around month three or four. Draw the bump and write the month onto the whiteboards on your display.

RESOURCES YOU WILL NEED FOR THIS LESSON

- ⌃ 'Two People Made Me' sensory story and associated resources

- ⌃ Images of a human embryo/foetus at monthly stages of development through pregnancy (you can find these online) – print month nine on A3 paper and then try to print the others to a suitable scale so that month one is very small

- ⌃ Modelling clay

- ⌃ Balloons (not blown up)

- ⌃ Baby product for lesson cue

PREPARATION

Set up the resources for the sensory story so they are within easy reach. Divide the modelling clay out between the tables.

OBJECTIVE

To ask 'how?' and 'why?' questions.

INTRODUCTION (15 MINUTES)

Cue the lesson using your chosen baby product.
Share the sensory story 'Two People Made Me' with the class.

GROUP TASK (10 MINUTES)

Revise the previous lesson by asking your students where babies grow. Allow a conversation to develop around the answer to this question and leave room for further questions to be asked. Elicit the question, 'How do babies grow?' from the group; a more accurate version of this question might be, 'How do babies change as they grow.'

Hand out the bump pictures and tell your students to look at them for clues. Allow students to chat to their neighbours and look at each other's pictures for clues. If someone notices that the bumps are different sizes, draw that to everyone's attention; if they don't, simply ask if someone has a picture of a small bump. Get the person with the small bump picture to stand on one side of the room and the person with the biggest bump picture to stand on the other side. The rest of your students can order themselves in between the biggest bump and the smallest bump in size order. If you have more pictures than students, they can deliver the images to their place in the line before returning to you to get another one.

Once you have a line of bump pictures arranged in size order, get your students to move along it from the small bump towards the big bump, indicating with their hands and arms how big they think their belly would be at the stages of pregnancy illustrated. As they walk down the line their hands go from being flat against their own stomachs to gradually moving away with their arms bowing until they make the shape of a large protruding belly.

INDIVIDUAL/GROUP WORK (20 MINUTES)

Add the bump photos to your display and look inside the woman on the display to see the baby that was placed there last lesson. During the coming 20 minutes you are looking for your students to make the link between the growing embryo/foetus and the growing stomach of the mother – in other words, to realise that the mother's stomach grows because the baby inside grows.

Remind the students that the baby starts off life inside the mother very, very small. If you are able to demonstrate the cell growing and dividing as described in the activity on page 168, you can do so; if it is too tricky or you do not have the right equipment, you can draw simple pictures on the board to show your students how the cell grows and divides.

Ask your students to take a small piece of clay from the lump on their table and roll it into a small ball to represent a single cell. As that cell grows they can add a little more clay from the lump. Once it is big enough to divide they can cut it in two and roll it into two small balls.

Allow them to continue this process until their lumps of clay are a decent size.

Ask your students what a baby looks like when it is born. You could use a baby doll or a picture to illustrate what a new-born baby might look like. Ask them to use the clay they have to model what they think a baby might look like before it is born.

Students who are unable to model clay can experience a progression of size. Use clay to represent the size of the embryo/foetus and a balloon to represent the size of the mother's tummy. Make a small ball of clay – the student can help to do this – and blow a balloon up to a small size. Allow the student to encounter these two examples of 'small'. Continue by making a larger ball of clay and blowing a balloon up slightly bigger than before, and keep going until you have the balloon blown up as far as it will go and a large ball of clay.

PLENARY (15 MINUTES)

Look at the models the students have made and show them the images of foetal development. Explain that at the start of pregnancy you would not be able to tell a woman was pregnant by looking at her. Write 'Month 1' on one of the whiteboards on your display and draw a side profile of a woman without a bump and place the one-month-old image of the embryo inside your paper woman. Cycle through the images for months two to four – you can invite students to update the whiteboards for you as you do this. End with your display woman at month five.

Share the sensory story 'Two People Made Me'.

Lesson plan 3: How does a baby get food? (1 hour)

This lesson provides a chance for you to highlight healthy eating messages for everyone.

RESOURCES YOU WILL NEED FOR THIS LESSON

- ⌃ 'Two People Made Me' sensory story plus sensory stimuli

- ⌃ A variety of food – both healthy and unhealthy

- ⌃ Baby product for lesson cue

Optional

- ⌃ A water spray and a bright torch

PREPARATION

Place the sensory stimuli where they will be easy to reach during the sensory story.

Display the food so that it is easy for students to see.

OBJECTIVE

To be able to identify healthy food.

INTRODUCTION (15 MINUTES)

Cue the lesson using your chosen baby product. Share 'Two People Made Me' with the class.

Update your display so that the woman pictured is now six months pregnant.

GROUP TASK (10 MINUTES)

Have all your students curl up in a small ball on the floor. If some students are unable to get down to the floor they can curl up small where they are or make a fist with their hands.

Tell your students that they are seeds waiting in the soil to grow. Ask them what they need to grow. Take the answer 'water' if it is offered and if not you can suggest it. You can spray them with the water spray to represent the seeds being watered (and because it will be fun). Once they have been watered your students can grow a little so that they are on their haunches with maybe their hands held a little way above their heads. Ask them what else they need to grow. You are looking for the answer 'sunlight'. Shine the torch to represent sunlight. Keep on watering and providing light until all your seeds are stretched up as tall as they can go – they are now fully grown plants.

INDIVIDUAL/GROUP WORK (20 MINUTES)

Explain to your students that babies growing inside the womb also need food and water to be able to grow. Tell them that the woman carrying the baby must eat food and drink water for the baby. Their task for this session is to decide what would be good for the woman to eat.

Students will make their decisions by exploring the food you have brought to the lesson – they can taste a little of the food, discuss it with their peers and with adults and research it on the internet and in books. When they decide that a food would be good for the woman to eat, students can either draw a picture or take a photograph of it.

Support your students in identifying healthy and unhealthy food. If a food they suggest is healthy, take their picture or photo and add it to the display on the classroom wall, positioning the food near the woman's mouth (if she has one) or on a dinner plate near the woman.

Students unable to make decisions about the food can explore healthy and unhealthy food using all their senses.

PLENARY (15 MINUTES)

Review your updated display and talk about the healthy foods your students have decided the woman should eat. Explain a little about what each of these foods will do for the baby, for example, 'She's going to drink milk – that will help the baby to develop strong bones.'

We know that the woman puts the food in her mouth, chews it and swallows it, but how does it get into the baby? Ask the students to look very closely at the picture of the baby inside the woman; can they spot anything that might be how the baby gets its food? If someone spots the umbilical cord, you can confirm that the baby gets nutrients from its mother through this cord.

Share 'Two People Made Me' together.

Lesson plan 4: What body parts does a baby have? (1 hour)

In this lesson students will look at the similarities between a baby's body and their own. They will begin to recognise that babies grow into children, who then grow into adults, and will think about what their bodies are capable of.

RESOURCES YOU WILL NEED FOR THIS LESSON

- ⌃ 'Two People Made Me' sensory story and resources
- ⌃ Music if you need it for the first task in the lesson
- ⌃ Tasks to be completed using different body parts, for example, a steady hand toy, a balance beam, food to eat
- ⌃ Baby product for lesson cue

Optional

- ⌃ The board game Twister.
- ⌃ Access to the internet and a selection of reference books.

PREPARATION

Set up the sensory story resources so that they are easily accessible as you share the story.

OBJECTIVE

To be able to name different parts of the body.

INTRODUCTION (15 MINUTES)

Cue the lesson using your chosen baby product and share 'Two People Made Me' with the class.

GROUP TASK (10 MINUTES)

Share a song that involves making actions together. Choose a song that names body parts, for example, the Hokey-cokey. For more streetwise students, chose a pop song that mentions body parts or actions done with specific parts of the body, consider The Macarena by Los del Rio, Willie and the Hand Jive by Johnny Otis, The Time Warp from *The Rocky Horror Picture Show*, or any song you can think of that mentions the actions of specific body parts.

An alternative to singing would be to play Twister!

INDIVIDUAL/GROUP WORK (20 MINUTES)

Update the woman on your display board so that she is seven months pregnant. Your students can help you to do this. Draw their attention to the baby inside of the woman – what body parts can they recognise?

During this section of the lesson students need to identify body parts common to themselves and the baby, for example, 'The baby has arms, I have arms,' identify what they can do with that body part, for example, 'I can use my arms to swim' and explore what the baby can do with the equivalent body part, for example, 'I do not know if a baby can swim.' Adults need to be on hand to guide the students in their explorations. It will also be handy to have access to the internet, for example, in the above example an adult could tell a student that there is fluid cushioning the baby inside the mother's womb, so they do move their arms through liquid, which is a bit like swimming, and they could show an online video of a baby swimming. Adults will need to think on their feet to extend the students' learning.

To prompt exploratory conversations you can challenge your students to complete the various body-part-specific tasks you have set up around the room or play Simon Says, reflecting on whether a baby could respond to the instruction.

PLENARY (15 MINUTES)

Ask the students if they discovered something that surprised them. (Perhaps that the baby drinks whilst in the womb – swallowing and urinating amniotic fluid.)

Share 'Two People Made Me' together.

Lesson plan 5: Does a baby have the same things inside it as we do? (1 hour)

In this lesson students will think about what is inside their bodies.

RESOURCES YOU WILL NEED FOR THIS LESSON

- ⋏ 'Two People Made Me' sensory story and resources
- ⋏ The book *Funnybones* by Janet and Allan Ahlberg, or an internet clip of the second song in the book, about which bones connect to which bones
- ⋏ Internet access and/or reference books
- ⋏ Large sheets of paper for drawing on and drawing materials for students
- ⋏ Baby product for lesson cue

Optional

- ⋏ Construction toys or clay

PREPARATION

Place the sensory resources ready to tell the sensory story.

Distribute the reference books and drawing materials amongst the tables.

OBJECTIVE

To begin to understand the functions of some internal organs.

INTRODUCTION (15 MINUTES)

Cue the lesson using your chosen baby product and share 'Two People Made Me' with the class.

GROUP TASK (10 MINUTES)

Update your display woman so that she is eight months pregnant. Remind your students that in the last lesson they thought about the parts of our bodies and the baby's body that we can see. Say that in this lesson they are going to think about body parts that we cannot see from the outside. Explain that we can feel these body parts.

Lead your students in some simple aerobic exercises, for example, jogging on the spot, star jumps, skipping, dancing, etc. Ask them to place their hand on their chest. They should be able to feel their own heart beating. Explain what they are feeling and that the heart pumps blood around the body.

INDIVIDUAL/GROUP WORK (20 MINUTES)

Working independently or in small groups, your students' task is to investigate what is inside their own bodies. Ask them to draw, or talk to someone about, what they think is there. Encourage students to feel their own hands and arms and to identify that there are bones beneath the flesh. Students who volunteer extra information, for example, that they have a stomach, can add these things to their drawings. You may find that some of your students have had operations and so have advanced knowledge about aspects of their body.

Students can use the internet and reference books to add information to their drawings.

Students unable to draw can discuss their ideas with an adult who can then draw for them or make a model, perhaps using construction toys or clay.

PLENARY (15 MINUTES)

Ask your students to share what they discovered about what is inside their bodies. Confirm that babies have the same things inside their bodies. Read or play an online video of the section from *Funnybones* about the bones connecting to one another.

Share 'Two People Made Me' together.

Lesson plan 6: What happens next? (1 hour)

This lesson encourages students to reflect on the baby's growth so far and to recognise that after it is born it should go on to grow into a young adult like themselves.

RESOURCES YOU WILL NEED FOR THIS LESSON

- ⅄ 'Two People Made Me' sensory story and associated resources

- ⅄ Pairs of images where one image shows an animal and the other shows its baby (internet clips can be a lot of fun to use – try baby giraffes!)

- ⅄ String and pegs

- ⅄ Card for drawing on and drawing materials

- ⅄ Baby product for lesson cue

- ⅄ Items from different stages of life – for example, a dummy, glasses, a driving licence – be mindful that some items that typically occupy a particular stage of life may not be so distinct for your students, for example, a walking stick is usually associated with old age but some students may need to use walking aids throughout their lives

PREPARATION

Ensure the sensory story resources are where you need them to be for sharing the story.

Spread the images of animals and their babies around the room – you can make this into a hide and seek activity to get your students using their observation skills and hide pictures up high, down low and in tricky places.

Hang the string so that it forms a line across your classroom that your students can easily reach. Have the pegs ready to use on the string.

OBJECTIVE

To understand that babies grow into adults and to begin to think about stages in the life cycle of humans.

INTRODUCTION (15 MINUTES)

Cue the lesson using your chosen baby product and share 'Two People Made Me' with the class.

GROUP TASK (10 MINUTES)

Update your display woman so that she is nine months pregnant. Ask your students what will happen next. Take the answer that the baby will be born. Your students may know about their own births and be able to contribute information about the different ways in which babies can be born.

Draw your students' attention to the animal images hidden around the room. Set them the task of finding pairs of animals – parent and young.

Establish that kittens grow into cats, eggs into chicks and then hens, tadpoles into frogs and so on. Share some internet clips if you wish.

Take the baby picture from the woman on your display (the baby is now born). Attach it with a peg to the start of the line strung across your classroom. Ask what the woman's baby will grow into and what will happen next.

INDIVIDUAL/GROUP WORK (20 MINUTES)

Working independently or in small groups, students must create a timeline for the average human life. They can do this by drawing pictures, writing words about each section of life or investigating and selecting objects to represent each stage of life.

Students can arrange their contributions in order on their tables.

PLENARY (15 MINUTES)

Bring everyone's contributions together and invite students to peg their creations on to the line in the correct order so that the sequence of birth, babyhood, childhood, teenage years, old age and eventually death is played out across the classroom. Allow students to offer their reflections on the cycle of life.

Share 'Two People Made Me' together for the final time.

TO THE CENTRE OF THE EARTH!

This story will place your story experiencer in a capsule and take them on an adventure to the centre of the earth. It has a repeating experience of vibrations through it, which is great for people who enjoy strong touch experiences.

Hold tight! We're starting the drills. We're going on a journey. We're going to drill all the way down to the centre of the earth.

Into the wet soil, through the roots of plants and trees, down we go!

We're drilling through rock now, burrowing through the earth's crust. Water drips through the cracks. Our drills are working hard.

What is this? Sticky, black and thick, it is oil! We journey on.

The drills continue through the hard mantle. The vibrations stop and we are tumbling forward through molten magma.

Our capsule is very hot now; see the control panel glowing red.

Look! The instruments on our control panel are spinning wildly: magnetic interference.

*Hear the drills beginning to bite again,
    grinding upon iron and nickel, we are
    approaching the earth's core. We're
    nearly there!*
*Suddenly we're weightless, drifting in the
    scorching centre of the earth. We are
    super humans to have survived this
    journey. Hurrah!*

About the story

Science fiction has often made the journey to the centre of the earth; Jules Verne's account is the most famous but many other authors have imagined the journey.

This story will work well for someone who uses a wheelchair with a tray attached. If your story experiencer is not a wheelchair user then sitting at a table can help you to create your capsule to adventure in. It is a very tactile story so may also suit someone with a sight or hearing impairment.

Resourcing the stimuli
Shopping list

- A tray with handles (ideally a metal one)

- A hand whisk or drill with a large chunky bit, for example, a square bit

- Wet soil, plant roots, fresh herbs

- Black food colouring, corn flour, water

- Water in a container that it can be slowly poured from

- Large gravel

- Red cellophane and a strong torch

- Cardboard, tinfoil, split pins, a felt-tip pen

Detailed list

> *Hold tight! We're starting the drills. We're going on a journey. We're going to drill all the way down to the centre of the earth.*

TOUCH, PROPRIOCEPTION AND SOUND

To create the vibrations in your imaginary capsule as you travel to the centre of the earth you are going to operate a hand drill or whisk between the table, or lap tray, and a tray with handles. If you are worried about scratching your table or lap tray, place a protective cloth over it before setting up for the story.

Ideally, the screen of the capsule will hide the hand whisk from the story experiencer, helping to preserve a little of the mystery of the adventure.

You may want to experiment with different ways of creating the drilling vibrations. If your story experiencer is able to hold onto the handles of the tray then they will prevent it from slipping off the table as you whisk or drill. If they are quite heavy handed then you will need a stronger drilling technique than if they have a lighter touch, for example, using a hand whisk underneath a tray whilst someone is pressing down hard will be tricky, but turning a hand whisk under a tray lightly balanced above it will be possible.

You are looking to make the tray vibrate and judder as if it is the control panel of a complex drilling machine. Whisks and drills offer a few options. Drill bits come in many different shapes and sizes; a square bit or a particularly lumpy bit will make creating vibrations easy. If you cannot get a hand whisk or a drill then you can try creating the vibrations in other ways, for example, putting a ridged surface below the tray and then pulling a large bead or ball on a string over it, which would produce vibrations. Another simple way of creating bumps and vibrations is to get two long lumpy sticks – you can make notches in wood, find sticks from the garden or two wooden spoons could even work. Cross them over one another between the tray and table in an X shape and move each back and forth to create bumps and vibrations. Creating the vibrations using this simpler method will not make the mechanical noise a drill or whisk will make. Depending on who your story experiencer is you may decide this is for the best because they will be able to focus on the story better without background noise, or you may choose to find a way of making a sound representing machinery to add atmosphere to the story – a hairdryer could create a gentle hum and also be useful later on when you want the capsule to get warmer.

Into the wet soil, through the roots of plants and trees, down we go!

TOUCH, SMELL AND TASTE

This is your best opportunity within this story to give your story experiencer smell and taste experiences. As your adventurer begins their journey they will be digging down through plants and soil to the rocks below; it is possible that surface plants would get tangled in the drill and be churned into the soil along with the roots and tubas of other plants. Create a tray of foliage or wet earth to explore. If you want the experience to be wholly edible then use mashed vegetables in place of earth. Adding fresh herbs such as lemon balm or mint will provide your story experiencer with smells as well as safe taste options.

If you are not aiming for taste then you can have lots of fun making an earthy exploratory tray with roots, twigs and root vegetables. If you are sharing the story with a dinosaur fan you might be able to add some pretend dinosaur bones or fossils to be discovered.

> *We're drilling through rock now, burrowing through the earth's crust. Water drips through the cracks. Our drills are working hard.*

TOUCH

Choose rocks that will not present a choking hazard if your story experiencer is likely to try and put them into their mouth. Be mindful that rocks can be thrown; if you think this is a possibility then choose smaller rocks or be ready to catch.

> *What is this? Sticky, black and thick, it is oil! We journey on.*

TOUCH AND TASTE

There are many ways to create a sticky goo. You can create a texture you think will interest your story experiencer. Remember that oil deposits hidden within the earth's crust may be contaminated with other particles, for example, sand and grit, so there is a lot of scope for creating a granular texture to your goo.

One of the simplest ways to create a goo is to use corn flour (in the USA corn flour is called cornstarch). To create the goo pour corn flour into a bowl, add a few drops of black food colouring and then gradually add water, stirring steadily until you reach a consistency you are happy with. If you want to create something that tastes a little nicer then use condensed milk instead of water – this will give you a thick, sticky, sweet, black goo. For an even simpler, even sweeter method, just use black treacle. You will get very sticky!

> *The drills continue through the hard mantle. The vibrations stop and we are tumbling forward through molten magma.*

TOUCH, VESTIBULATION AND SOUND

The drill vibrations will be created in the same manner as in the first section of the story. To create the sensation of tumbling you can encourage or support the story experiencer to move in a tumbling manner; this could be by rolling over on the floor or by moving in loops and circles. If your story experiencer is a wheelchair user then you may be able to steer their wheelchair in loops for them; if they are able to drive their chair it can still be good for you to control it for this part of the story, as the adventurers in the capsule would have no control of its tumbling as it falls through the viscous lower mantle and molten outer core.

Our capsule is very hot now; see the control panel glowing red.

SIGHT AND TOUCH

To make the control panel on your capsule glow red, shine a torch with red cellophane over the front at it. If you are using a hairdryer to create a machinery noise along with your drilling, you can allow the heat from the hairdryer to warm up the tray that is being used as the base of your story experiencer's control panel. As there is no drilling for this part of the story, you could also warm the tray by placing a hot water bottle between the tray and the table – this would also create the rocking sensation of tumbling through dense molten fluid. The centre of the earth reaches temperatures similar to those on the sun; clearly you will not want to expose your story experiencer to dangerously hot things so be careful if you are using boiling water in the hot water bottle or a hairdryer (hold your hand under the flow of air to check the heat, and remember that a temperature that seems bearable can become too hot over time).

Look! The instruments on our control panel are spinning wildly: magnetic interference.

SIGHT, TOUCH AND PROPRIOCEPTION

Making your control panel can be a lot of fun, and it may be something you want to spend some time doing with your story experiencer before setting off on your journey. To create a simple capsule make a curve or fold of cardboard that can be stood in front of the tray or even attached to it. This can be like the dashboard in a car with a number of dials on display low down, or you can let your imagination run wild and build a capsule from cardboard boxes big enough to actually climb inside, with windows and buttons. The dials are the important part for this stimulus. The earth's magnetic fields are believed to be caused by currents in the metal of the core of the earth – at this part of your journey you would be within that core and the currents would be all around you, so the magnetic field would not be as stable as it is on the surface of the earth. This magnetic instability would interfere with electronics and so it is likely that the dials in your capsule would spin. To create a spinning dial, mark a circle on the card and notch and number it around the edge so that it could be recording speed or depth. Make a needle out of strong card that will point to the speed or depth. Attach the needle to the centre of the circle using a split pin and turn it a few times to make sure that it will spin easily. You can wrap or glue tin foil around your dial, or over your needle, to make it look like a metallic instrument.

> *Hear the drills beginning to bite again, grinding upon iron and nickel, we are approaching the earth's core. We're nearly there!*

TOUCH AND SOUND

Create the vibrations of the drill in the same manner as before.

> *Suddenly we're weightless, drifting in the scorching centre of the earth. We are super humans to have survived this journey. Hurrah!*

PROPRIOCEPTION, VESTIBULATION AND SOUND

Weightlessness would be a very tricky thing to create unless you happen to be sharing the story on the moon or indeed at the centre of the earth. So rather than weightlessness itself we are going to aim for movements similar to those performed by people in zero gravity. If you have ever seen footage of astronauts moving about inside space capsules you will have noticed that their movements are slow and deliberate – they glide and drift. You can be as creative as you like here, but a simple approach would be to have your story experiencer raise their hands (you can support them to do this if they need help). Once their arms and hands are raised they can sway and even spin as if they are drifting and weightless.

Surviving such a journey is impossible, as temperatures at the centre of the earth reach over 9,000°F, so to have made it successfully you and your story experiencer really must be super human in some way. These super powers and the success of your journey are worth cheering about, so you can end the story by cheering loudly together.

Facilitating the stimuli

Hold tight! We're starting the drills. We're going on a journey. We're going to drill all the way down to the centre of the earth.

Have your story experiencer hold on to the handles of the tray, as if they were safety handles inside their capsule. If they are unable to grasp the handles then simply resting their hands on the tray will work.

Create the vibrations in whichever manner you have chosen.

If you are creating a supporting sound, make sure it is loud enough and located in a place where you and the story experiencer will both be able to hear it. You do not want to have to shout the story because you are being drowned out by the noise of the drill…or maybe you do (but if you do, remember this is a story that is intended to be retold so you might earn yourself a sore throat over time).

Into the wet soil, through the roots of plants and trees, down we go!

Place the tray of soil and plants on top of the tray that is being used as your capsule; allow the story experiencer time to explore its contents and give them time to take in its smells.

We're drilling through rock now, burrowing through the earth's crust. Water drips through the cracks. Our drills are working hard.

Exchange the tray of soil and plants for rocks. It may be easier for you to have these on a tray too. You can wet the rocks before giving them to the story experiencer; keeping them in cold water can be good, as the story experiencer will experience the contrast between the warmth of natural fibres and earth and the coolness of stone. Alternatively, you can gently drip water onto the story experiencer's hands as they touch the rocks, as if water were dripping from rocks above them.

What is this? Sticky, black and thick, it is oil! We journey on.

Trade the rocks for a bowl of gloop and allow time for its exploration. It will probably be handy to have a damp cloth and towel on hand for the end of this experience. Remember that, for your story experiencer, having their hands cleaned and dried is as much a sensory experience as touching sticky goo. Aim to ensure consistency in this experience, just as you would with the others.

The drills continue through the hard mantle. The vibrations stop and we are tumbling forward through molten magma.

Facilitate the drilling stimuli in the same way as before. You can choose to vary the drilling, for example, slow drilling and high-pitched, fast drilling, etc., or to make it consistent throughout the story. It is likely that your choice will be based on the needs of your story experiencer. If you are looking for your story experiencer to be able to anticipate the sensation of drilling then you might want to keep the experience consistent over the story and over different tellings.

Our capsule is very hot now; see the control panel glowing red.

Be sure that the parts of the control panel that the red light falls upon, or lights up, are in a position where they are easy for your story experiencer to feel.

If you have placed a hot water bottle underneath the tray or are directing the flow of air from a hairdryer towards it, allow enough time for the tray to heat up and then enough time for your story experiencer to process the sensation of heat beneath their hands.

Look! The instruments on our control panel are spinning wildly: magnetic interference.

Make the dial spin by giving it a good push with your fingers; this can be fun to do and you may want to encourage or support your story experiencer to spin the dials for themselves – this will help them to develop their awareness of where their body is in space as they coordinate their senses of sight and proprioception to move their hand towards the needle.

If you want to be really cunning you could attach a paper clip to the end of your needle and use a magnet hidden behind the control panel to cause the needles to move. If you are particularly dedicated to detail you could have a magnet present during the whole story and gradually move the needle around to show different depths or speeds as you progress towards this part of the story and then move the needle rapidly to indicate the magnetic disturbance. This can be a fun job for a sibling or friend of the story experiencer to be given.

Hear the drills beginning to bite again, grinding upon iron and nickel, we are approaching the earth's core. We're nearly there!

Repeat the drill vibration experience, varying it or keeping it consistent as is appropriate to your story experiencer.

> *Suddenly we're weightless, drifting in the scorching centre of the earth. We are super humans to have survived this journey. Hurrah!*

If your story experiencer is able to make the weightless movements themselves then make them with them – you are both in the capsule and you are both weightless, so enjoy it!

If your story experiencer will need your support to make the movements then be sure that you know enough about their range of movements to facilitate the movements without hurting them. You can try making smaller movements at first and warming up to larger waving motions.

Exploration activities

There are many sensory experiences to be explored within this story. You can choose to explore one on each telling of the story, select favourites or experience them in sequence. Here are some ideas of things you might like to try.

The earth's surface

Growing on the earth's surface: Before the capsule begins its journey to the centre of the earth it is perched on the earth's surface – picture it surrounded by flora and fauna. Selecting edible plants and flowers and using these to create a cover of greenery over an object representing the capsule will offer your explorer the chance to experience their scents, textures and even flavours as they search for the capsule within. Use a deep bowl or a bucket to hide the capsule so that it cannot immediately be seen.

Mud, mud, glorious mud

Grown-ups might not be so keen on mud unless they are at a beauty salon, but mud can be a fabulous touch experience and with a bit of splatting and delving about it also becomes a sound experience too. You can buy child-friendly compost or clay or simply use mud from the garden. Creating different consistencies of mud will make this experience more interesting for your story experiencer, so try some sloppy, runny mud and some thick, gloopy mud, Dress head to toe in waterproofs if you need to – be a bold adventurer unafraid of getting messy!

Temperature

The capsule gets hotter as it journeys deeper into the earth. You need to be very careful of not using things that are too hot, and be aware that some people are more sensitive to temperature than others, but by using a selection of cool and warm items you will be able to create the experience of different temperatures. Think about using: ice cubes, warm water, hand warmers, a hairdryer and cold metal.

You could also explore:

- Things that spin, like the instruments as the capsule reaches the centre of the earth. Find a selection of spinning toys – even spin yourself – and use them to explore what spinning means.

- Make your own super-duper dashboard with lots of different knobs, buttons, switches and dials on it. You can make these using bottle tops and cardboard or find real ones from a junk shop or hardware shop.

Creative activity

Layers

The capsule sets out to discover what is underneath the earth's surface. You can create art from discovering what is underneath the surface of a picture. Colour a piece of paper or card with lots of bright colours or use brightly coloured or metallic paper to begin with. Cover your paper with a layer of thick wax crayon, and then use a retractable biro with its nib retracted to draw into it, scratching off the crayon to reveal the colours underneath.

Create your own world using layers of papier mâché. Begin with a water balloon (blow it up and tie it but do not put water in it). Tie the balloon on a string and hang it somewhere where it will be low enough for you to work on it. You might need to put newspaper or protective sheeting underneath the balloon to catch any drips.

A simple way to make papier mâché is to mix a solution of flour and water and then soak strips of newspaper in it. Wrap the soaked newspaper around the balloon until it is completely covered. Leave it to dry.

You are going to add lots of layers to your balloon, but you need to wait until each is dry before adding the next. Think about ways to make your layers different.

- ⅄ You could scrunch up dry newspaper and use your papier mâché to stick it to the balloon. This would create lumps and hills on your balloon.

- ⅄ You could colour your papier mâché with powder paints or food colouring.

- ⅄ You could add glitter or sand to your papier mâché to create texture.

- ⅄ You could dip wool or string into your flour and water and wrap these around your balloon.

- ⅄ Invent your own layers.

When you have added as many layers as you want, wait until they are all completely dry, and then explore what they look like when you open your balloon up. You may be able to use a saw to cut your layered balloon in half; you may be able to dig into its surface as if you are the capsule in the story.

Discovery activities

Research

Make a list of all the different materials the capsule encounters on its journey to the centre of the earth. Use books and the internet to find out what we use all these materials for.

Vibrations

The drill causes the capsule to vibrate, and sound is formed by vibrations in the air. Explore a range of musical instruments and try to identify which part of them vibrates to cause the sound.

Journey

Go on a journey of your own and try to notice the same sorts of things that are noticed in the 'To the Centre of the Earth!' story. Think about: what do you see, what sounds do you hear, is any machinery involved in your journey, what temperature is it at the start, middle and end of your journey, do you feel bumps or vibrations?

Six lesson plans for 'To the Centre of the Earth!'

Although the journey in the story is a fantasy, it still provides a lot of scope for learning science. This series of lesson plans all follow the scientific method in their format; by repeating this method students will develop an understanding of a scientific way of thinking. The different substances encountered on the journey to the centre of the earth provide these lessons with a starting point for thinking about and identifying different types of materials. Lessons about temperature, magnetism and forces could also be built upon the back of this story. These lessons imagine that your students are the scientists who undertook the journey and now that they have returned safely to the earth's surface they are undertaking experiments to learn more about what they encountered.

Using the scientific method with students with learning disabilities

The cue to all of these lessons is a song that is intended to get students thinking about the purpose of science. It is sung to the tune of 'An English Country Garden'; the tune has natural pauses (indicated with a * in the text of the song below). It can be fun to punctuate these pauses with a particular action – a clap or something of your own invention. I always enjoyed using an air cannon with my students – shooting it at a different individual in each pause!

THE SCIENCE SONG

> *How many things can we find out, in this our science **
> *lesson?*
> *There is so much to learn about the world and science*
> *helps us ** learn it.*

Looking and listening, tasting and smelling, touching
and asking lots of questions,
We can do-o all these things in this our science * lesson!

The scientific method involves taking our initial understanding of a topic and using this to form a question/theory that we would like to discover the answer to/test. Scientists use their initial understanding of the topic to make a prediction as to what the outcome of their experiments will be.

To test a scientific theory relies upon an understanding of variables – everything stays the same and one thing is changed.

Scientists observe closely, and record, the outcomes of changing one variable.

It is hoped that the experiment will answer the question. Scientists then look to explain why the answer is as it is; they reflect on their experiment to see if it could be done better and decide what they want to find out next.

To run the scientific method within a lesson you will need to use the headings:

- ⋏ Question

- ⋏ Prediction

- ⋏ Same/different

- ⋏ Results

- ⋏ Answer

Your students will reflect on each of these titles as they progress through the lesson. In some lessons you will be providing the question; in others students can come up with their own. You will then discuss how to find out the answer to your question. It may be that you present a way of doing this; it may be that students can design a way themselves. Once the 'how' of your experiment has been established with your students, you will identify the variables. What will stay the same? What will change? Next you need to have a discussion to establish how you are going to record the results: drawing, photos, tally chart, numerical recording, etc. Your students will then carry out the experiment. Once you have gathered the data together you can look at it and see if you have answered your question. Then you can reflect on why you got the answer you did, how you might do the experiment better next time and what you would like to find out next.

This can seem complicated, but students of all ages and abilities, with support, can meaningfully follow the scientific method.

Lesson plan 1: Planting herbs and spices (1 hour)

In this lesson students will plant herbs and learn about where fruit and vegetables come from. The lesson will also serve as an introduction to the structure of the scientific method, which is going to permeate this whole series of lessons.

If your students enjoy this lesson you might like to explore the free resources provided by Grow Your Own Potatoes.[6]

RESOURCES YOU WILL NEED FOR THIS LESSON

- The sensory resources linked to the story

- Compost or cotton wool, seeds for quick-growing herbs, for example, cress

- Pots to grow your herbs in

- Small bits of plant, small pictures of fruit and vegetables

- A watering can or suitable item for watering plants

- A selection of fruit and vegetables – ideally put these in a large bucket with a blanket over the top, or a large cardboard box with a small hole cut in the side so that children will be able to reach in and feel the items without seeing them

- Access to the internet or pre-printed images of the fruit and vegetables you have chosen growing in their natural environments

PREPARATION

Make sure you can reach all the resources for the sensory story as you need them. Place the kits to plant herbs on tables around the room where you will send groups to work. Have the internet available (or your pictures ready) and your fruit and vegetables stashed near you.

---

6   These are available by clicking the link to educational resources on my website http://jo.element42.org./.

OBJECTIVE

To gain an understanding of where our food comes from.

Question: Where do fruit and vegetables come from?

INTRODUCTION (15 MINUTES)

Sing the science song to cue the lesson. Share the 'To the Centre of the Earth!' sensory story. Explain that the lesson is going to be focused on a question. You can reinforce the concept of a question by signing 'question' – to do this form your forefinger and thumb into a circle, and then imagining that they are holding a pen, draw a question mark in the air in front of you. Establish what your students already know about where fruit and vegetables come from – support them in answering that they are grown.

GROUP TASK (10 MINUTES)

This is a movement-based game to energise everyone and to allow any wriggles to come out before the table task.

To play the game each student takes a turn at selecting an item of fruit or vegetables from the box. Take this opportunity to invite them to explore their senses – what does it feel like? Take it out – what does it smell like? If appropriate, you could let them taste it. They could pass it around the group so everyone gets to experience it.

Cue the movement by saying, 'This is a… ! Show me where it grows, ready, steady, and grow!'

Students must form themselves into a shape that represents where the item grows – for example, on a tree or underground. You can support students in this activity by showing pictures of the plants growing.

Show an image of the vegetable or fruit growing in its natural environment so everyone can see if they got the answer right. For students with sight impairments, you can speak the answer or offer them a tactile answer, for example, a touch of earth, grass or a stem of a plant (or branch of a tree).

Students who are unable to answer for themselves can experience this activity through their proprioceptive, vestibular and touch senses – first touching the vegetable and then experiencing the movement of their body as they are supported in giving the answer physically.

Summarise at the end of the game: we know that fruits and vegetables grow, and grow in lots of different places, but we do not know where they come from. Remind students of the question they are answering. Perhaps someone will offer the prediction: 'seed'.

Ask students how they could find out. If they are able to provide the answers, let them do so; structure their thinking with the questions you ask. If they do not have the information, provide it yourself. You are looking to establish that we can find out whether a plant grows from a seed by planting a seed and seeing whether a plant grows. Perhaps plants grow from something else, such as small parts of plants, perhaps pictures of plants.

Display the labels 'Same' and 'Different'.

Under 'Same' list or display what will be the same for all the plants – each one will have a pot, each one will have soil and each pot will be watered.

Under 'Different' list or display what is going to change – changing what we plant, seeds, plant pieces, pictures, etc.

INDIVIDUAL/GROUP WORK (20 MINUTES)

Students can work on their own or in small groups, whichever suits them best, to plant seeds and the other items. Try to enable students to do this as independently as possible, for example, some students may be able to complete the whole task on their own if you give them a simple prompt sheet; others may need physical support to do the planting but will not need telling what to do. Make sure any adults working with the students focus on supporting them to be as indipendent as possible.

Students experiencing this activity on a purely sensory level can be allowed plenty of time to explore the feel of the soil and its smell, as well as the sound of the seeds in their packets and the feeling of them being sprinkled on their skin.

Water the plants once they are planted and explain that everyone will be looking after their plants every day from now on.

PLENARY (15 MINUTES)

Explain when the students will be able to answer their question. Establish how you will record the results (taking photos of the pots each day is a simple way to do this).

Share the sensory story 'To the Centre of the Earth!' together.

Try to make time to come back and view the results of your experiment at a later date.

Lesson plan 2: Water experiment (1 hour)

In this lesson students will discover what water can pass through. Your students will also have their understanding of the scientific method reinforced.

RESOURCES YOU WILL NEED FOR THIS LESSON

- ⅄ The sensory resources linked to the story

- ⅄ Water

- ⅄ Cups

- ⅄ A water tray or outside area that can get wet

- ⅄ Various materials to form lids on the cups, for example, tissue paper, paper, card, plastic, wood, tin foil, fabric, etc.

Optional

- ⅄ A sheet of rubber or P-seal tape (you can find this in hardware shops), rubber bands

PREPARATION

Ensure the story resources are within easy reach. Place cups and lid materials in the water tray or outside.

Apply P-seal around the rims of all the cups so that when they are pressed against the lids there will not be any leaking at the edges. A circle of rubber cut to be the same size as the rim of the cup and sandwiched between the cup and the lid can also serve this purpose. For flexible lids a rubber band around the top of the cup can also help to make a good seal. If you opt not to use a seal like this then you need to highlight to your students that they are looking for water passing through the lid, not slipping out the crack between the lid and the cup around the edge.

OBJECTIVE

To practise using the scientific method.

Question: What can water get through?

INTRODUCTION (15 MINUTES)

Sing the science song to cue the lesson. Share the 'To the Centre of the Earth!' sensory story. Return to the line of the story that mentions water passing through the cracks in rock. Show an image of water running through a crack. Ask students if the water is running through the rock. Lead them in understanding that the water is only able to go through the cracks, not the rock. You can show them this using a cup and a rock lid (a slate tile is an easy option here). Introduce this lesson's question to them and ask them to make predictions.

GROUP TASK (10 MINUTES)

Display a chart listing all the lid materials that you have. Have a column on the chart for predictions and one for results; you could also have a final wider column for explanations. Explain to your students that they are going to predict which materials water will be able to pass through. They will be playing the part of water. Have all your students move to one side of the classroom and hold up one of the lid materials. If the students think water could pass through that particular material then they should move past it to the other side of the classroom; if they think water could not pass through the material they should stay where they are or stop moving once they draw level with the material. Your students can add detail to their predictions with how they move, for example, running quickly through tissue paper or wriggling slowly through wood. Record their predictions on your chart.

INDIVIDUAL/GROUP WORK (20 MINUTES)

To run the experiment students should fill a cup with water, place a lid on it and then turn it over to see if water passes through the lid. Before they begin their experiment, have them identify the variables in a 'Same' and a 'Different' column. 'Same' will be the water and cup; 'Different' will be the lid.

Encourage students to record what happens in any way that suits them.

PLENARY (15 MINUTES)

Gather everyone's data and add it to the large chart. Talk about how the experiment went. Take ideas from students about why some materials let water through and others do not. Ask them to imagine they were going on a different adventure, this time in a boat across the sea. Based on the knowledge they learned today, what would they build a boat out of and why?

Share 'To the Centre of the Earth!' together once more.

Lesson plan 3: Describing materials (1 hour)

In this lesson your students will increase their vocabulary of scientific descriptor words.

RESOURCES YOU WILL NEED FOR THIS LESSON

- ⅄ The sensory resources linked to the story

- ⅄ A variety of different substances, for example, water, custard, glue, jelly, tin foil, cling film, fabric, velvet, Velcro, wood, glass, metal, etc.

PREPARATION

Set up the sensory story resources. Hide three substances in boxes near you. Spread the different substances out around the room.

OBJECTIVE

To gain an appreciation of the different textures of various substances and to develop related vocabulary.

Question: What does it feel like?

INTRODUCTION (15 MINUTES)

Sing the science song to cue the lesson. Share the 'To the Centre of the Earth!' sensory story. Go back to the sticky oil touch experience. Ask students to describe how it feels – encourage expressive vocabulary.

GROUP TASK (10 MINUTES)

Show your students the three boxes with different substances hidden inside. Invite one student to come to the front of the room to feel inside a box. They must describe what they feel inside but not name the object. The other students must guess what is in the box. You can support them by giving them samples to touch; they can choose the object they think is being described.

Ask students to look around the room at all the substances that you have laid out. Can they decide on a question for the lesson, for example, 'What does it feel like?' or 'What feels sticky?' Your students can focus on different questions.

Make the 'Same' and 'Different' lists. 'Same' would be touching (you are not describing how things taste or smell, unless that is your question); 'Different' would be what you touch.

INDIVIDUAL/GROUP WORK (20 MINUTES)

Conduct individual experiments. Record results in a manner that suits you.

PLENARY (15 MINUTES)

Share questions and answers. Ask students what else they would like to find out - your next lesson will be based upon their ideas!

Share the sensory story 'To the Centre of the Earth!' together.

Lesson plan 4: Student choice (1 hour)

In this lesson students will work on their own questions and experiments.

RESOURCES YOU WILL NEED FOR THIS LESSON

- ⌃ The sensory resources linked to the story

- ⌃ Whatever resources are required by your students' planned experiments

PREPARATION

Lay out the sensory story resources within reach. Prepare the resources your students will need.

OBJECTIVE

To use the scientific method to answer a question.

Question: Students' own. (These can be sourced from those generated during the previous lesson's plenary or taken from those generated during the introductory activity in this lesson.)

INTRODUCTION (15 MINUTES)

Sing the science song to cue the lesson. Share the 'To the Centre of the Earth!' sensory story. Discuss the questions students will be working on.

GROUP TASK (10 MINUTES)

Work together to identify the variables in each experiment, completing the 'Same'/'Different' lists.

INDIVIDUAL/GROUP WORK (20 MINUTES)

Conduct individual experiments and record their results.

PLENARY (15 MINUTES)

Report back to the class on the outcome of each experiment. Celebrate all that has been found out.

Share the sensory story 'To the Centre of the Earth!' together.

Lesson plan 5: Temperature (1 hour)

In this lesson students will measure temperature in informal and formal ways.

RESOURCES YOU WILL NEED FOR THIS LESSON

- The sensory resources linked to the story
- Warm water
- Ice cubes
- Hot water bottle
- Tea light candle in a narrow-necked glass jar
- Metal
- Fur
- Other items of various temperatures – be mindful of safety and do not select anything that could harm students
- Thermometers

PREPARATION

Set up sensory story resources and distribute other items across the tables.

OBJECTIVE

To gain an understanding of temperature as scalar.

Question: How hot is it?

INTRODUCTION (15 MINUTES)

Sing the science song to cue the lesson. Share the 'To the Centre of the Earth!' sensory story. Talk about how the capsule gets hotter as it gets closer to the centre of the earth. Have students think of a question for the lesson.

GROUP TASK (10 MINUTES)

Have students each stand near an item. Upon your instruction they must walk to a different item in the room. Give instructions based on temperature, for example, walk to something hotter, walk to something that feels cold, walk to something a little bit hotter and walk to something warm, etc.

INDIVIDUAL/GROUP WORK (20 MINUTES)

Demonstrate how to use a thermometer. Students will be measuring the temperature of the different items around the room and recording – independently or with support – their temperature numerically and also descriptively, for example, 'warm' or 'very hot'.

Before everyone begins experimenting, complete the 'Same'/ 'Different' lists together.

PLENARY (15 MINUTES)

Have all the students look at their results – together you are going to rank the items in order of temperature from coldest to hottest. Discuss safety implications of extreme temperatures: hot items can burn you; when it is very cold it is important to wrap up warm.

Share the sensory story 'To the Centre of the Earth!' together.

Lesson plan 6: Magnetism (1 hour)

In this lesson students will be introduced to the concept of magnetism and will learn what items are magnetic.

RESOURCES YOU WILL NEED FOR THIS LESSON

- ⅄ The sensory resources linked to the story
- ⅄ Bar magnets
- ⅄ A selection of materials – plastic and metal bottle tops, paper clips, tin cans, wooden pencils, etc.

PREPARATION

Set up the resources for the sensory story within easy reach.
Distribute the materials around the room.

OBJECTIVE

To discover magnetism.
Question: What is magnetic?

INTRODUCTION (15 MINUTES)

Sing the science song to cue the lesson. Share the 'To the Centre of the Earth!' sensory story. Talk about what happens to the instruments as the adventurers reach the centre of the earth. Explain that the instruments are normally turned by the mechanism inside but that a stronger force from outside is overpowering the internal mechanism. Tell the students that the name of this force is magnetism.

GROUP TASK (10 MINUTES)

Hand out the magnets; explain that magnets only work on some things. Invite students to explore their environment with the magnets. (Be sure to protect anything that you are worried about the magnets touching.)
Invite students to come up with a question to investigate using the magnets e.g. 'Is my schoolbag magnetic?', 'Is my chair magnetic?'. Complete the 'Same'/'Different' lists.

INDIVIDUAL/GROUP WORK (20 MINUTES)

Students should complete their experiments and record their results. A fun experience for students can be to sort small materials on a thin plastic tray by holding a magnet underneath and dragging items that magnetise to one end of the tray.

PLENARY (15 MINUTES)

Share findings and report on how the experiments went.
Share the sensory story 'To the Centre of the Earth!' together. Celebrate all you have discovered during the journey of sharing 'To the Centre of the Earth!'

THE FOREST OF THORNS

Original text by Gwendolen Benjamin, based on the tale of 'Sleeping Beauty'.

'It is an old tale, your majesty,' said the attendant, 'from an old time, when fairies still walked the world.'

'At the heart of that forest lies a cursed princess, who pricked her finger on a spindle and was sent to sleep for one hundred years.'

Naturally, the prince's duty was to rescue this damsel but several hours of clambering through the forest of thorns had put a damper on his initial burst of heroics.

Wizened trunks twisted into a heavy canopy that blocked out the sunlight and a century of fallen leaves rotted underfoot.

He knew fairies did not exist anymore, but he was followed by a strange chittering and shadows danced at the edges of his vision.

Sweating in grimy armour, his arms grew heavier each time he swung his sword.

He sat heavily on a root and a burst of sunlight caught his eye amongst the oppressive grey of the forest.

It illuminated a rosebush that had somehow found its way out of the mulch, in full bloom and cheerfully unaware of its surroundings.

The prince hacked his way through another briar patch.

He wasn't sure he could give the sleeping princess happily ever after, but he could start by giving her a rose.

★

THE FOREST OF THORNS

Simplified version, adapted from Gwendolen Benjamin's original.

A long time ago, when fairies still walked
the world.

A princess pricked her finger on a spindle
and fell asleep for one hundred years.

Naturally, the prince's duty was to rescue
this damsel but several hours of
clambering through the forest of thorns
had put a damper on his initial burst of
heroics.

Wizened trunks twisted into a heavy canopy
that blocked out the sunlight and a
century of fallen leaves rotted underfoot.

He knew fairies did not exist anymore, but
he was followed by a strange chittering
and shadows danced at the edges of his
vision.

Sweating in grimy armour, his arms grew
heavier each time he swung his sword.

He sat heavily on a root and a burst of
sunlight caught his eye amongst the
oppressive grey of the forest.

It illuminated a rosebush that had somehow found its way out of the mulch, in full bloom and cheerfully unaware of its surroundings.

The prince hacked his way through another briar patch.

He wasn't sure he could give the sleeping princess happily ever after, but he could start by giving her a rose.

Author Gwendolen Benjamin has created a new version of the traditional tale of 'Sleeping Beauty' especially for this book. In her story you will find a prince who shows remarkable determination when faced with the challenge of a forest of thorns he must hack through in order to rescue his princess. The prince's persistence in confronting difficulty is a great message to share with your students. The fantasy elements of the story lend themselves well to the creation of magical sensory experiences for your story experiencers.

Resourcing the stimuli
Shopping list

- Glitter

- Paper (sliver paper)

- A heavy blanket

- Rose scent (perfume, essential oil, potpourri, a strong smelling flower)

- Salt and a mild herbal tea bag

- A rose (ideally a fresh one, but a fake one would be good for consistency)

- A torch (or daylight in a room that can be dulled e.g. by drawing curtains)

Optional

- A few metal coat hangers or a musical instrument to create a fairy sound

Detailed list

> *'It is an old tale, your majesty,' said the attendant, 'from an old time, when fairies still walked the world.'*

SIGHT

Glitter: Choosing an iridescent or pearlised colour of glitter, or mixing several different colours of glitter together, will create a more magical effect than a single bold colour. A low lamp or an LED light source can be used to accentuate the sparkling of the glitter. An alternative to glitter would be to use an indoor sparkler to dance before the story experiencer's eyes.

TOUCH

Roll a sheet of paper to form a point that is safe to use against someone's skin. Choosing silver paper will make your paper point more needle like.

> *Naturally, the prince's duty was to rescue this damsel but several hours of clambering through the forest of thorns had put a damper on his initial burst of heroics.*

MOVEMENT

This experience is going to be delivered through the story experiencer's body so you need nothing more than for them to be present.

> *Wizened trunks twisted into a heavy canopy that blocked out the sunlight and century of fallen leaves rotted underfoot.*

SIGHT/SMELL

For this experience you can choose between using a heavy blanket or decomposing leaf matter.

A heavy blanket will be used to form the canopy of leaves overhead. You can of course create the darkness of the blocked out sunlight in other ways, by turning the lights off in a room where you can achieve blackout for example, but if you are able to use a weighty blanket then you can facilitate your story experiencer's understanding of the word 'heavy.'

Decomposing leaf matter gives off a forest like scent. If you do not want to use foliage that is actually decomposing try choosing something that is naturally fragrant, pine needles for example. If you do not have a garden you can borrow from then you will be able to find foresty aromas in places that sell potpourri.

> *He knew fairies didn't exist anymore, but he was followed by a strange chittering and shadows danced at the edges of his vision.*

SOUND

You can create a chittering noise with your voice, or choose a musical instrument that you think suits the sound of fairies. If you want to make an instrument yourself, experiment with shaking small beads inside a glass jar or small balls of tin foil in a metal bowl. Jangling a handful of metal coat hangers also makes a magical tinkering sound suitable fairy chittering. If working with a group you could explore sounds in a session before beginning to tell the story and invent a chittering noise all of your own, after all who knows what fairies sound like?

> *Sweating in grimy armour, his arms grew heavier each time he swung his sword.*

TOUCH/ TASTE

Add a teaspoon of salt to a cup of hot water. Rip open a herbal tea bag and add the contents to your concoction.

> *He sat heavily on a root and a burst of sunlight caught his eye amongst the oppressive grey of the forest.*

SIGHT

Use a bright torch to be the shaft of sunlight, or better yet, tell the story in a room which you can make dull by drawing the curtains and let in a real shaft of sunlight at this point (of course this relies on there being sun outside!)

> *It illuminated a rosebush that had somehow found its way out of the mulch, in full bloom and cheerfully unaware of its surroundings.*

SMELL

Finding a rose scent should be easy, many perfumes have a rose base, essential oils and potpourri also offer rose scents in abundance. Think about how you are going to store and replenish the scent over multiple tellings of the story. If using potpourri keep the bag sealed and pour out a little fresh each time you tell the story. If using essential oil add a couple of drops to a cotton pad and store it in a plastic container, allowing the air inside the container to become fragranced. Many perfumes change their smell over time, and are designed to be smelt on skin, so you may have to use yourself as the smell and spray a little onto your hand. Think about whether you will be wearing the scent through the whole story

– this would be appropriate as the prince hacking through the forest might be able to smell the roses in the distance. If you are going to wear the smell through the whole story consider wearing it on your left hand and keeping that hand back as you facilitate the other stimuli and then presenting it for this section so that there is a marked change in the experience.

The prince hacked his way through another briar patch.

MOVEMENT

As with the prince's earlier endeavours all you need for this experience is your story experiencer.

He wasn't sure he could give the sleeping princess happily ever after, but he could start by giving her a rose.

SIGHT/SCENT/TOUCH

Being handed a rose is not necessarily a big sensory experience, a rose is relatively small in our field of vision, unless we get pricked by a thorn (and hopefully you will not be) it is not a big touch experience, and scents vary. You can do your best to make this rose a good sensory experience by choosing one with a bold colour, ensuring it has a strong scent - you could cheat by adding a few drops of essential oil or a spritz of perfume if you think it needs it, and presenting it against a contrasting background. Consider wearing clothes that will make it easy for your story experiencer to see the rose against, e.g. if you wear a white t-shirt and hold a red rose in front of you that is going to be a bigger visual experience than if you are wearing a floral top in various pink tones and holding up a rose.

Facilitating the stimuli

'It is an old tale, your majesty,' said the attendant, 'from an old time, when fairies still walked the world.'

Sprinkle glitter across the vision of the story experiencer. If you sharing the story in a room with dull light, having a low lamp beneath the gaze of the story experiencer can make the glitter twinkle more.

'At the heart of that forest lies a cursed princess, who pricked her finger on a spindle and was sent to sleep for one hundred years.'

Prick the finger of your story experiencer with the paper point. If your story experiencer is able they can mime falling asleep in response to this.

Naturally, the prince's duty was to rescue this damsel but several hours of clambering through the forest of thorns had put a damper on his initial burst of heroics.

Move your story experiencer's legs as if they are clambering. Be aware of their movement range and facilitate this experience in a way that is appropriate to them. If your story experiencer is able to move their own limbs then they can mime clambering through the forest themselves.

Wizened trunks twisted into a heavy canopy that blocked out the sunlight and century of fallen leaves rotted underfoot.

Hold the heavy blanket over the head of your story experiencer, you can allow it to droop so that some of its weight presses against them. It is entirely appropriate for them to have to lift their hand and push it away so as to be able to see. Or allow your story experiencer time to take in the scent of the decomposing leaf matter.

He knew fairies didn't exist anymore, but he was followed by a strange chittering and shadows danced at the edges of his vision.

The fairies are all around the prince but he does not see them. Create the sound of chittering using your voice, coat hangers, or the instrument of your choosing or creation. Move the sound around to create the impression of the fairies dancing about.

Sweating in grimy armour, his arms grew heavier each time he swung his sword.

Rub some of the salty tea onto your story experiencer's arm. The small particles of herb provide the feeling of the grime against the skin, and the salt will add the taste of sweat should the grime be tasted. Be aware that consuming too much salt is dangerous. One teaspoon in a cup of fluid should not present a problem, but make sure your story experiencer does not treat the cup as a drink.

He sat heavily on a root and a burst of sunlight caught his eye amongst the oppressive grey of the forest.

Use your torch to create a burst of light, or draw back the curtains in your darkened room.

It illuminated a rosebush that had somehow found its way out of the mulch, in full bloom and cheerfully unaware of its surroundings.

The rose bush is still at a distance from the prince. From where he is he can see it in the light and catch its scent on the breeze. You could allow the rose stimulus from the final line of the story to be visible as you waft the scent of roses under the nose of your story experiencer. Make sure you allow enough time for them to take in the scent. Do not encourage story experiencer's to sniff vigorously as this actually makes our smell weaker. We smell as the scent crosses sensors in our nasal passageways, sniffing vigorously makes the scent pass by faster so we have less chance of smelling it. Normal breathing, or even slow gentle breathing through the nose, is the best way to pick up a scent.

The prince hacked his way through another briar patch.

Move your story experiencer's limbs as if they are hacking through the briar patch. If your story experiencer is able to move their own limbs then they may mime this action. You can choose whether to match this experiencer to the previous physical experience, or whether to create a contrasting experiencer. Matching the experiencer would mean that on both occasions you assist your story experiencer in moving their legs as if clambering. Creating contrasting experiencers would meant that on the first occasion you would support your story experiencer in moving their legs and on this line you would support them in creating a hacking motion with their arms.

He wasn't sure he could give the sleeping princess happily ever after, but he could start by giving her a rose.

Hand your story experiencer the rose. Position yourself so that your story experiencer gets the maximum impact from this exchange (see the description in the detailed stimuli list on page 217 for further information).

Exploration activities

In 'The Forest of Thorns 'the prince struggles to get through the forest. All of these exploration activities involve making your way from A to B; various sensory adventures await you.

Fairy footsteps

Create a set of sensory steppingstones by placing items of different textures on the floor. You can place items directly onto the floor or secure them to carpet tiles or cardboard to keep them together. Here are some suggestions:

- sand
- corrugated cardboard with the corrugated bit displayed
- pasta of all different shapes and sizes, cooked and uncooked
- fur fabric
- velvet
- beads in a bag
- cushions.

Sprinkle a thin trail of glitter between the steppingstones and have your story experiencer follow in the fairy footsteps. If you have more than one story experiencer you could place the steppingstones quite far apart and lay different trails using different coloured glitter.

Optional extension: create some sensory glitter play at the end of the trail of fairy footsteps for your story experiencer to explore, try sprinkling glitter into a water-play tray with a few drops of food colouring, filling a water bottle with water and glitter to shake like a snow globe or adding glitter to a tray of shaving foam.

For individuals who are unable to walk, make a fingertip fairy footstep journey by gluing items of different textures onto a large sheet of cardboard and marking a route with glitter.

Clambering journey

This exploration is great for individuals who are able to propel themselves along the floor but are not able to walk. Collect pillowcases or duvet covers and fill them with different textured items, for example:

- cuddly toys
- pasta
- dried peas
- scented draw liners
- a little talcum powder
- bells
- cord, rope or electrical wire (without the plug on)
- cushions
- balls
- balloons.

Lay the filled pillowcases and duvet covers around on the floor, cover them with different textures of fabric if you have them and allow your story experiencer to have their very own clambering sensory adventure as they move around the room.

Chittering experiences

It is great to include your story experiencer in creating and setting up this experience. Use your imaginations to think of what sort of sound a chittering might be. Set up a route lined with noise-making items. Follow the route and hear the different sounds along it. The items might be:

- plastic bottles filled with different items, dangling on strings
- milk bottle tops, or swatches of tin foil, thread onto cotton and dangling alongside each other
- bead curtains or chain curtains
- bells

⅄ wind chimes

    ⅄ metal coat hangers

    ⅄ empty plastic bottles with their lids on and another empty bottle to hit them with

    ⅄ sand in a container to roll along

    ⅄ lentils, split peas, dried peas or pasta in a container to roll or shake

    ⅄ a coin in a glass jar to roll or shake

    ⅄ rubber bands of different sizes stretched around a box or margarine tub

    ⅄ balloon rubber stretched over the top of bottles, tins, pots, etc., held down with strong rubber bands or duct tape, to tap with the fingertips

    ⅄ glass beakers filled with different amounts of water to be hit gently with a teaspoon

    ⅄ beads on a string to be dragged over a selection of metal, plastic and glass containers

    ⅄ cardboard tube rainmakers – a cardboard tube with straws poked through it and a handful of rice sealed inside it.

Creative activities

Make armour

Create your own armour – this can be as basic or adventurous as you like. For basic armour use masking tape to secure cardboard boxes or tin foil packets to your body. For more adventurous armour spend time designing and creating tin-foil-covered cardboard pieces for yourself – consider bib-shaped card structures to form chest armour, tubes to cover the forearms and the shins, shields and even swords.

Once you have your armour on pretend to be the prince. Go outside and hack through the forest of thorns until your armour is sweaty and grimy.

Make a diorama

In the story a shaft of sunlight illuminates a rose growing in a clearing in the forest of thorns. You can make a diorama of this scene using a shoebox, some dull coloured card, a green pipe cleaner and a little bit of red or pink tissue paper.

- ⅄ Cut a variety of tree shapes out of your cardboard. Make sure your trees are not taller than the shoebox, and leave a little bit of extra card on them at the bottom, which can be folded over and used to secure the trees into the shoebox.

- ⅄ Make two holes in the shoebox: one on the smallest end of the box and one in the lid of the box in the centre about one third of the way along the lid.

- ⅄ Use tape or glue to stick your trees into the shoebox, leave a space where the light from the hole in the lid will fall.

- ⅄ Use the pipe cleaner and tissue paper to make a rose and attach it in the clearing in your cardboard forest.

- ⅄ Seal the lid onto the box and use the second hole as a viewing hole.

Once you have made the basics of your diorama you could improve it by adding extra little slits into the box to create a little bit of light in other areas of the forest. You could make grass by snipping the edge of paper to fray it and gluing it in. Try covering the extra holes you create with coloured cellophane (happily, some chocolates come wrapped in cellophane wrappers so it may be necessary to eat sweets whilst you do this) - you might be able to create a murky green light in some areas of your diorama and a shaft of golden sunlight above the rose.

Discovery activities

What happened in the beginning?

Gwen's version of the story begins with the princess already slumbering. Find out about how she came to fall asleep by researching the start of the 'Sleeping Beauty' story.

What happens next?

There is a little known second part to the story: once the princess wakes up, she and the prince are married and have children but the wicked queen mother tries to have the children cooked so she can eat them for her dinner. Find out what happens by researching this part of the 'Sleeping Beauty' story.

What happens in other stories?

Find out about other fairy tales that have trapped princesses in them and spot things that are the same and different between them and this tale. For example, in 'The Forest of Thorns' the princess is trapped in sleep, in 'Rapunzel' the princess is trapped in a tower and in both stories princes rescue the princesses. Write your own story with some elements that are the same as and some that are different from 'The Forest of Thorns'.

To whom would I give a rose?

The prince wants to give the princess a life lived happily ever after, but he knows the best he can do in the moment is to give her a rose. Draw a rose in the middle of a sheet of paper and around it draw the people you would like to make happy. Make a rose and give it to someone you would like to make happy.

Six lesson plans for 'The Forest of Thorns'

At the time of writing, the National Curriculum for literacy in the UK requires that students encounter retellings of traditional folk and fairy stories in their studies. Over the course of these six lessons your students will have the opportunity to encounter and explore a retelling of the story of 'Sleeping Beauty'. They will be given opportunities to explore themes from the story, as well as expressing preferences about and respond imaginatively to the story.

Lesson plan 1: Exploring the story (1 hour)

This lesson will give your students the opportunity to explore the story and think of how one of its themes is acted out in their own lives.

RESOURCES YOU WILL NEED FOR THIS LESSON

- ⅄ 'The Forest of Thorns' sensory story and associated resources

- ⅄ Items pertinent to your students' own struggles (see lesson content for further information)

- ⅄ A sleeping sound clip (you can find clips of people snoring gently on YouTube, you could create gentle snoring noises yourself or you could use a gentle sleepy tune)

PREPARATION

Ensure the resources for telling the sensory story are set out in such a way that they will be easily accessible as you tell the story. Place the resources for specific students at the tables they will be working at.

OBJECTIVE

To explore the story and its relevance to our own lives.

INTRODUCTION (15 MINUTES)

You will cue in each lesson in the same way; you have some choices about how to do this, so decide what will most suit your class and what will be easy for you to deliver.

- ⅄ Play the sleeping clip.

- ⅄ Fall asleep yourself near your chair in the circle – students need to follow your lead and move over to the circle to fall asleep by their chairs (you can play the sleeping clip along with this).

- ⅄ Dim the lights and play the sleeping clip.

Once everyone is in the circle with you, share 'The Forest of Thorns' sensory story.

GROUP TASK (10 MINUTES)

Ask your students to identify the events of the story. Do they think the story is true or made up? Use the terms 'fiction' and 'non-fiction' with them. Explain that together you are going to act out the story as they remember it. You have two options of how to do this.

1. Ask all of the students to join you on one side of the room and explain that they are the prince, and the princess is asleep on the other side of the room. What do they have to do to get there? Mime hacking through the forest together and discovering the rose.

2. Choose one student to be Sleeping Beauty, one to be the prince and one to be the rose bush; everyone else has to pretend to be trees. Arrange the students so that Sleeping Beauty is on one side of the room and the prince on the other, with the trees and rose bush in between. The prince must then hack his way through the trees (who can sit down as they are chopped down), find the rose and present it to the sleeping student.

INDIVIDUAL/GROUP WORK (20 MINUTES)

Students can work alone or in small groups. Support your students in recognising that the prince had to try very hard to achieve his goal. Give each student a task that they have to try hard at to achieve. Try to choose activities pertinent to that student, such as things they have recently struggled to do. Ask them to approach the activities as if they are the prince and to keep on trying.

Consider a wide range of activities when selecting things for your students to persist at; you could choose a task from another lesson or you could choose a task that is not directly related to work, for example, playing collaboratively with another child, sharing nicely, eating food without making a mess or using a walking frame.

PLENARY (15 MINUTES)

Talk about the different activities that students have been doing, remind everyone how hard the prince tried in the story and praise them for trying hard like the prince.

Share 'The Forest of Thorns' sensory story together.

Lesson plan 2: Recognising the retelling (1 hour)

In this lesson students will discover that 'The Forest of Thorns' is a retelling, if they have not already recognised that, and they will identify common characters, events and settings between the various retellings of the story.

RESOURCES YOU WILL NEED FOR THIS LESSON

- ⅄ 'The Forest of Thorns' sensory story and associated resources

- ⅄ Books, videos, cassette tapes, etc. that show retellings of *Sleeping Beauty*

- ⅄ Sleeping sound clip

PREPARATION

Make sure the resources for the sensory story are laid out ready for you to share the story.

Prepare each student a sheet of paper divided into two columns and as many rows as you have alternative versions of 'Sleeping Beauty' for them to explore (this may be different for different students depending on your expectations of how many versions they can consider in one lesson). Label the columns 'Same' and 'Different'.

Place the alternative versions of 'Sleeping Beauty' at different locations around the room.

Prepare symbols for students who are going to complete the main task using symbol communication.

OBJECTIVE

To identify features of a story, for example, characters, events and settings.

INTRODUCTION (15 MINUTES)

Cue the lesson and share the sensory story as you did in Lesson 1.

GROUP TASK (10 MINUTES)

Create an instant role-play of your very own school-based version of 'Sleeping Beauty', involving your students as actors as you go along. Move about as you do this – if you have members of staff supporting you then you might be able to use different locations in the school (you might even be able to co-opt non-teaching staff into helping out). Here is an example:

Once upon a time the head teacher pricked her finger on a drawing pin and fell asleep.

Class 2 were expecting a visit from the head teacher and when she did not arrive they began to get worried. They decided to go and find her.

They put their work and toys away.

They put on their coats.

They looked all around the playground.

They looked in the assembly hall.

They looked in the head teacher's office and there she was. (Peer through the window to see the head teacher slumped over her desk asleep, with a drawing pin nearby.)

They tried to get into the office but the door was very heavy – they had to push and push and push.

Eventually they got in and woke the head teacher up with a big… (your students can fill in their own response).

Ask your students if their role-play is the same as 'The Forest of Thorns'. It is likely that some people will say yes and some no. Working with your students, identify aspects that were the same and aspects which were different.

INDIVIDUAL/GROUP WORK (20 MINUTES)

Working individually or in small groups students should move from one location in the room to another. In each location they will encounter a retelling of the story of 'Sleeping Beauty' and will be expected to fill in on their sheets things in that story that were the same as 'The Forest of Thorns' and things that were different. Students who use alternative forms of communication can be supported to fill in the sheets, for example, they can sign to a scribe who fills in the sheet on their behalf or they can use symbols or pictures to identify similarities and differences.

PLENARY (15 MINUTES)

Have everyone look at their sheets – can you find one thing that all the stories had in common?

Share 'The Forest of Thorns' sensory story together.

Lesson plan 3: What if? (1 hour)

This lesson is going to ask students to consider the gender roles in the story and use their imagination to think about how the story might have gone if things had been the other way around for the prince and princess.

RESOURCES YOU WILL NEED FOR THIS LESSON

- ⊼ 'The Forest of Thorns' sensory story and associated resources
- ⊼ Role-play clothes
- ⊼ Drawing materials
- ⊼ Sleeping sound clip

PREPARATION

Place the sensory resources for the story where they will be easily accessible during the telling of the story.

Create four distinct locations in the room, each for a different type of story exploration: role-play, drawing, writing and talking.

OBJECTIVE

To respond imaginatively to a story.

INTRODUCTION (15 MINUTES)

Cue the lesson and share the sensory story as before.

GROUP TASK (10 MINUTES)

Divide the class into boys and girls. Have the boys go to one side of the room and the girls to the other. Ask one person to demonstrate something they are good at; they can mime this activity, for example, a boy might come forwards and mime kicking a football. Ask the rest of their group if they too can do that activity and any who can should join in the mime. Then ask the whole room whether this is an activity just for boys. Any girls who can also kick footballs would now join in the mime. Repeat a few times until everyone gets the idea that what we can do is rarely dependent on our gender.

INDIVIDUAL/GROUP WORK (20 MINUTES)

Ask the class to imagine what would have happened in the story if it were the prince who had fallen asleep and the princess who had performed the rescue.

Invite students to pick an area of the room to work in (let them know that they will work in two locations during the lesson so if there are too many people in one spot they can be reassured that they will get a turn).

Students who choose writing or drawing may wish to have the whole of the time in one space.

Students should work in their chosen locations to imagine what might happen in the role-reversed version of the story.

Half way through the group work time, ask students to move to a fresh location.

PLENARY (15 MINUTES)

Find out what students thought might have happened with the princess performing the rescue.

Share 'The Forest of Thorns' sensory story together (you could subtly switch the characters, keeping the story exactly the same but having the male and female roles reversed in response to the lesson).

Lesson plan 4: Dreams (1 hour)

In this lesson students are going to be given free rein to explore their imaginations and run with what they come up with.

RESOURCES YOU WILL NEED FOR THIS LESSON

- ⅄ 'The Forest of Thorns' sensory story and associated resources
- ⅄ Sleeping sound clip
- ⅄ Role-play, drawing and writing resources

PREPARATION

Set up the room in the same way as the previous lesson.

OBJECTIVE

To respond to a story imaginatively.

INTRODUCTION (15 MINUTES)

Cue the lesson and share the sensory story.

GROUP TASK (10 MINUTES)

Involve students in acting out what they do at the end of a day, for example, brush my teeth, put my pyjamas on, get into bed, read/have a bedtime story, shut my eyes and sleep.

Once everyone is pretending to be asleep, ask them what happens next. If someone answers that they get up, ask them what happens before that. Find the answer, 'I dream.'

Ask everyone to lie still and quietly, and to think about what they might be dreaming if they were asleep.

Take some examples of dreams from students. Students can communicate their dreams to you in any way they find easy, for example, verbally, using signs, pointing at images or acting them out.

INDIVIDUAL/GROUP WORK (20 MINUTES)

Students choose locations to work in as with the previous lesson; this time their task is to imagine what the sleeping princess (or prince if they choose) dreams about.

Half way through the session students may swap to explore their imaginations in a different location in the room, using a different form of expression. You can encourage students to work with, or alongside, different peers when they change locations.

PLENARY (15 MINUTES)

Explore the students' imagined dreams. Ask them why they thought those dreams might be dreamed.

Share 'The Forest of Thorns' again together.

Lesson plan 5: Read, recite and act (1 hour)

By now your students are familiar with 'The Forest of Thorns'; some may even know it by heart. In this lesson they can come to realise for themselves how much they have learned and demonstrate it through reading, recitation and acting.

RESOURCES YOU WILL NEED FOR THIS LESSON

- ⋏ 'The Forest of Thorns' sensory story and associated resources

⮝ Sleeping sound clip

⮝ Copies of the text of 'The Forest of Thorns' (with symbol/pictorial support where appropriate)

⮝ Extra sets of the sensory resources used in the telling of 'The Forest of Thorns'

PREPARATION

Set up the resources for the sensory story so that they are easy to reach for anyone telling the story.

Set up three locations in the room for working in, one for reading, one for reciting and one for role-play.

Place texts of the sensory story in the reading location, make sure there is a clear space in the role-play location, and place the extra set of sensory resources in the recitation location (students unable to read, or unable to speak can recite the story by sharing the sensory experiences in sequence).

OBJECTIVE

To read, recite and act out familiar stories.

INTRODUCTION (15 MINUTES)

Cue the lesson as usual.

Ask if any of the students feel able to lead the sharing of the sensory story. If someone does then hand over the role of teacher to them at this point and assume the role of a student sharing in the sensory story.

GROUP TASK (10 MINUTES)

Explain that sometimes we remember things because we practise them a lot and try hard to remember them – for example, our times tables or bringing our PE kit to school on Tuesdays – and at other times we just remember things without even noticing we have remembered them. Choose some singing and movement games to illustrate this point, for example do your students know the words to and how to do the 'Hokey-cokey' or 'Ring a Ring' o' Roses'? If your students are older they might know the words to a favourite pop song or the moves to a particular dance. Choose one of these combinations of singing and movement to do together.

INDIVIDUAL/GROUP WORK (20 MINUTES)

In this part of the lesson students are going to discover what they already know. As with previous lessons, students have the choice of four locations to work in and can swap locations part way through the task if they wish.

Students in the role-play location must act out 'The Forest of Thorns' as accurately as they can.

Students at the reading location must see if they can read the story independently.

Students in the recitation location can see if they can remember the words to the story and say them out loud (or sign them or use any form of communication appropriate to them).

Students using the sensory resources should communicate their recitation through the sensory narrative of the story, as opposed to the verbal one.

PLENARY (15 MINUTES)

Find out if the students were able to remember the story and ask them to demonstrate what they were able to achieve during the lesson.

Share the sensory story together; again you may hand over the teacher role or you can ask students to facilitate a section each.

Lesson plan 6: My favourite part (1 hour)

This is the final lesson on 'The Forest of Thorns'; students will be familiar with the story by now and I hope they will have enjoyed the work they have done exploring the story. This lesson is their chance to express their opinions about the story and their work.

RESOURCES YOU WILL NEED FOR THIS LESSON

- ⋏ 'The Forest of Thorns' sensory story and associated sensory stimuli
- ⋏ Sleeping sound clip
- ⋏ Examples of work from previous lessons or a record of work from previous lesson (perhaps you took photographs to record what the students were doing)
- ⋏ Writing materials
- ⋏ Drawing/painting/collaging materials

PREPARATION

Make sure the sensory story resources are to hand for the telling of 'The Forest of Thorns'.

Set up four locations in the room for writing, talking, role-play, drawing and painting, etc.

OBJECTIVE

To express preferences.

INTRODUCTION (15 MINUTES)

Cue the lesson in the same way as previous lessons.

Share the sensory story together. You may hand over the lead role in the sharing to a student if you have a student capable of taking on the role from you.

GROUP TASK (10 MINUTES)

Set your students the task of telling you whether they like or dislike various items. With each item they must convey their like or dislike in a manner you specify.

Begin with familiar items, and then progress to people and events in 'The Forest of Thorns'.

Here are some ways of expressing like/dislike you could ask your students to use.

- ⚲ 'Show me whether you like or dislike this using thumbs up or thumbs down.'

- ⚲ 'Show me using just your face.'

- ⚲ 'Show me using just your body.'

- ⚲ 'Show me by saying a sentence with an adjective in.'

INDIVIDUAL/GROUP WORK (20 MINUTES)

Students can choose which one of the four work locations they work in and have the option of switching locations as usual. You may want to encourage students to use locations they have not previously used.

There are two questions to be answered:

1. What has been your favourite piece of work we've done on 'The Forest of Thorns' and why?

2. What is your favourite part of 'The Forest of Thorns' and why?

If a student wishes to do an extended piece of work, for example, a long piece of writing or a detailed picture, they can choose to spend the whole session answering just one question. If they prefer to switch work locations then they can switch questions too.

PLENARY (15 MINUTES)

Find out what everyone has enjoyed about exploring the story of 'The Forest of Thorns' and what they liked about the story. Be sure to check their reasons for their favourite parts and encourage other students to discuss whether they liked that part too and if not, why not?

Share 'The Forest of Thorns' together for the final time.

References

Anderson, K., Bird, M., Macpherson, S., McDonough, V., Davis, T. (2010) 'Findings from a pilot investigation of the effectiveness of a Snoezelen Room in Residential Care: Should we be engaging with our residents more?' *Geriatric Nursing, 32*, 3, 166–177.

Anonymous (2006) 'Email forum: Ice breaking.' *PMLD Link 18*, 3, 55, 35.

Ayer, S. (1998) 'Use of multi-sensory rooms for children with profound and multiple learning disabilities.' *Journal of Learning Disabilities for Nursing, Health and Social Care 2*, 2, 89–97.

Boucher, J. and Bowler, D. (2011) *Memory in Autism: Theory and Evidence.* Cambridge: Cambridge University Press.

ten Brug, A., van der Putten, A., Penne, A., Maes, B. and Vlaskamp, C. (2012) 'Multi-sensory storytelling for persons with profound intellectual and multiple disabilities: An analysis of the development, content and application in practice.' *Journal of Applied Research in Intellectual Disabilities 25*, 350–359. Available at http://onlinelibrary.wiley.com/doi/10.1111/j.1468-3148.2011.00671.x, accessed 30 July 2014.

Bruner, J. S. (1959) 'The cognitive consequences of early sensory deprivation.' *Psychosomatic Medicine 21*, 2, 89–95.

Dunn, W. (1997) 'The impact of sensory processing abilities on the daily lives of young children and their families: a conceptual model.' *Infants and Young Children 9*, 4, 23–35.

Dunn, W. (2007) 'Supporting children to participate successfully in everyday life by using sensory processing knowledge.' *Infants and Young Children 20*, 2, 84–101. Available at http://depts.washington.edu/isei/iyc/20.2_dunn.pdf, accessed 30 July 2014.

Empson, J. (2012) *Rabbityness.* Wiltshire: Child's Play (International).

Fava, L., Strauss, K. (2009) 'Multi-sensory rooms: Comparing effects of the Snoezelen and the stimulus preference environments on the behaviour of adults with profound mental retardation.' *Research in Developmental Disabilities, 31*, 160–171.

Gabbard, C. and Rodrigues, L. (2007) 'Optimizing Early Brain and Motor Development Through Movement.' *Early Childhood News.* Available at www.earlychildhoodnews.com/earlychildhood/article_view.aspx?ArticleID=360, accessed 20 June 2014.

Glenn, S. (1987) 'Interactive Approaches to Working with Children with Profound and Multiple Learning Difficulties.' In B. Smith (ed.) *Interactive Approaches to the Education of Children with Severe Learning Difficulties.* Birmingham: Westhill College.

Gray, G. and Chasey, C. (2006) 'SMILE: a new service development for people with profound and multiple learning disabilities.' *PMLD Link 18*, 3, 55, 27–31.

Hayes, S., McGuire, B., O'Neill, M., Oliver, C. and Morrison, T. (2011) 'Low mood and challenging behaviour in people with severe and profound intellectual disabilities.' *Journal of Intellectual Disability Research 55*, 182–189. Available at http://onlinelibrary. wiley.com/doi/10.1111/j.1365-2788.2010.01355.x, accessed 30 July 2014.

Hussein, H. (2010) 'Using the sensory garden as a tool to enhance the educational development and social interaction of children with special needs.' *Support for Learning 25*, 1, 24–31.

Jarrold, C., Nadel, L. and Vicari, S. (2008) 'Memory and neuropsychology in Down syndrome.' *Downs Syndrome Education Online.* Available at www.down-syndrome.org/ reviews/2068/, accessed 20 June 2014.

Kingsley, E. P. (1987) *Welcome to Holland.* Available at http://www.our-kids.org/Archives/ Holland.html, accessed 30 July 2014.

Lacey, P. (2006) 'Inclusive literacy.' *PMLD Link: Changing Perspectives 18*, 3, 55, 11–13.

Lacey, P. (2009) 'Developing the thinking of learners with PMLD.' *PMLD Link: Sharing Perspectives 21*, 63, 15–20.

Lacey, P. (2011) 'Listening to challenging behaviour.' *PMLD Link: Speaking up, Being Heard 23*, 1, 68, 7–10.

Longhorn, F. (1988) A Sensory Curriculum for Very Special People: A Practical Approach to Curriculum Planning. London: Souvenir Press.

McCormack, B. (2003) 'Snoezelen: A mother's story.' *The Exceptional Parent, 33*, 10, 38–41.

Murray, M., Hudson Barker, P., Murray-Slutsky, C., and Paris, B. (2009) 'Strategies for supporting the Sensory-Based Learner.' *Preventing School Failure Heldref Publications, 53, 4*, 245–251.

Ockenden, J. (2006) 'The development of a culture of engagement in a service supporting adults with profound and multiple learning disabilities.' *PMLD Link: Changing Perspectives 18*, 3, 55, 3–8.

Owen, J. P., Elysa J., Marco, E. J., Desai, S., Fourie, E., Harris, J., Hill, S., Arnett, A., Mukherjee, P. (2013) 'Abnormal white matter microstructure in children with sensory processing disorders.' *NeuroImage: Clinical 2*, 844–853. Available at www.sciencedirect. com/science/article/pii/S2213158213000776, accessed 30 July 2014.

Parker, A. T. (2011) 'Supporting friendship development for students with low-incident disabilities.' *Impact 24*, 1, 10–11.

PAMIS (2002) *Real Lives: Real Stories – Summary of results developing literacy skills through multi-sensory story-telling in children and young people with profound and multiple learning disabilities* [Brochure].

Piaget J. (1952) *The Origins of Intelligence in Children.* M. Cook, translator. New York: International Universities Press.

Pollitt, K. (1991) Hers; The Smurfette Principle. *The New York Times.* Available at http://www.nytimes.com/1991/04/07/magazine/hers-the-smurfette-principle.html, accessed 30 July 2014.

Raphael, C. and Clark, M. (2011) 'Christian.' *PMLD Link 23*, 1, 68, 18–20.

Swanson, L. H. (1993) 'Working memory in learning disability subgroups.' *Journal of Experimental Child Psychology 56*, 1, 87–114.

Vlaskamp, C. and Cuppen-Fonteine, H. (2007) 'Reliability of assessing the sensory perception of children with profound intellectual and multiple disabilities: A case study.' *Child: Care, Health and Development 33*, 5, 547–551.

Vlaskamp, C., Hiemstra, S. J. and Wiersma, L. A. (2007) 'Becoming aware of what you know or need to know: Gathering client and context characteristics in day services for persons with profound intellectual and multiple disabilities.' *Journal of Policy and Practice in Intellectual Disabilities, 4*, 2, 97–103.

Young, H. and Lambe, L. (2011) 'Multi sensory story telling for people with profound and multiple learning disabilities.' *PMLD Link 23*, 1, 68, 29–31.

Further Reading

Carpenter, B. (1992) 'A post-16 educational project for students with profound and multiple learning difficulties.' *International Journal of Adolescence and Youth 3*, 3, 4, 363–371.

Champagne, T. and Stromberg, N. (2004) 'Sensory approaches in inpatient psychiatric settings: innovative alternatives to seclusion and restraint.' *Journal of Psychological Nursing 42*, 9, 34–44.

Devlin, S., Healy, O., Leader, G. and Huges, B. (2011) 'Comparison of behavioral intervention and sensory-intergration therapy in the treatment of challenging behavior.' *Journal of Autism and Developmental Disorders 41*, 1303–1320.

Gerrad, S. and Rugg, G. (2009) 'Sensory impairments and autism: A re-examination of casual modelling.' *Journal of Autism and Developmental Disorders 39*, 1449–1463.

Lane, A., Dennis, S. and Geraghty, M. (2011) 'Brief report: Further evidence of sensory subtypes in autism.' *Journal of Autism and Developmental Disorders 41*, 826–831.

Lane, A., Young, R., Baker, A. and Augley, M. (2010) 'Sensory processing subtypes in autism: association with adaptive behavior.' *Journal of Autism and Developmental Disorders 40*, 112–122.

Longhorn, F. (2011) 'A short history of shout, glow, jump, taste, smell, touch and wobble: Multi-sensory education (part 2).' *PMLD Link 23*, 1, 68, 29–31.

McNicholas, J. (2000) 'The assessment of pupils with profound and multiple learning disabilities.' *British Journal of Special Education 27*, 3, 150–153.

Minshew, N. and Hobson, J. (2008) 'Sensory sensitivities and performance on sensory perceptual tasks in high-function individuals with autism.' *Journal of Autism and Developmental Disorders 38*, 1485–1498.

O'Konski, M., Bane, C., Hettinga, J. and Kruli, K. (2010) 'Comparative effectiveness of exercise with patterned sensory enhanced music and background music for long-term care residents.' *Journal of Music Therapy 47*, 2, 120–136.

Park, K. (2004) 'Interactive storytelling: from the Book of Genesis.' *British Journal of Special Education 31*, 1, 16–23.

Simmons, B. (2011) *The 'PMLD Ambiguity': Articulating the Lifeworlds of Children with Profound and Multiple Learning Difficulties.* Paper presented at: the Nordic Network on Disability Research (NNDR) 11th Annual Conference, Reykjavik, Iceland (28 May 2011).

Simmons, B. and Bayliss, P. (2007) 'The role of special education for children with profound and multiple learning difficulties: is segregation always best?' *British Journal of Special Education 34*, 1, 19–24.

Taylor, J. (2006) 'Using multi sensory stories to develop literacy skills and to teach sensitive topics.' *PMLD Link: Changing Perspectives 18*, 3, 55, 14–16.

Thurman, S. (2011) 'Is communication a human right for people with profound and multiple learning disabilities?' *PMLD Link: Speaking Up, Being Heard 23*, 1, 68, 10–15.

Index